Aspects of Unity in J. S. Bach's Partitas and Suites

Eastman Studies in Music

Ralph P. Locke, Senior Editor, Eastman School of Music

(ISSN 1071–9989)

The Poetic Debussy: A Collection of His Song Texts and Selected Letters (Revised Second Edition)
Edited by Margaret G. Cobb

Concert Music, Rock, and Jazz since 1945: Essays and Analytical Studies
Edited by Elizabeth West Marvin and Richard Hermann

Music and the Occult: French Musical Philosophies, 1750–1950
Joscelyn Godwin

"Wanderjahre of a Revolutionist" and Other Essays on American Music
Arthur Farwell, edited by Thomas Stoner

French Organ Music from the Revolution to Franck and Widor
Edited by Lawrence Archbold and William J. Peterson

Musical Creativity in Twentieth-Century China: Abing, His Music and Its Changing Meanings (includes CD)
Jonathan P. J. Stock

Elliott Carter: Collected Essays and Lectures, 1937–1995
Edited by Jonathan W. Bernard

Music Theory in Concept and Practice
Edited by James M. Baker, David W. Beach, and Jonathan W. Bernard

Music and Musicians in the Escorial Liturgy under the Habsburgs, 1563–1700
Michael Noone

Analyzing Wagner's Operas: Alfred Lorenz and German Nationalist Ideology
Stephen McClatchie

The Gardano Music Printing Firms, 1569–1611
Richard J. Agee

"The Broadway Sound": The Autobiography and Selected Essays of Robert Russell Bennett
Edited by George J. Ferencz

Theories of Fugue from the Age of Josquin to the Age of Bach
Paul Mark Walker

The Chansons of Orlando di Lasso and Their Protestant Listeners: Music, Piety, and Print in Sixteenth-Century France
Richard Freedman

Berlioz's Semi-Operas: Roméo et Juliette *and* La damnation de Faust
Daniel Albright

The Gamelan Digul and the Prison Camp Musician Who Built It: An Australian Link with the Indonesian Revolution
Margaret J. Kartomi

"The Music of American Folk Song" and Selected Other Writings on American Folk Music
Ruth Crawford Seeger, edited by Larry Polansky and Judith Tick

Portrait of Percy Grainger
Malcolm Gillies and David Pear

Berlioz: Past, Present, Future
Edited by Peter Bloom

The Musical Madhouse (Les Grotesques de la musique)
Hector Berlioz, Translated and edited by Alastair Bruce
Introduction by Hugh Macdonald

The Music of Luigi Dallapiccola
Raymond Fearn

Music's Modern Muse: A Life of Winnaretta Singer, Princesse de Polignac
Sylvia Kahan

The Sea on Fire: Jean Barraqué
Paul Griffiths

"Claude Debussy As I Knew Him" and Other Writings of Arthur Hartmann
Edited by Samuel Hsu, Sidney Grolnic, and Mark Peters
Foreword by David Grayson

Schumann's Piano Cycles and the Novels of Jean Paul
Erika Reiman

Bach and the Pedal Clavichord: An Organist's Guide
Joel Speerstra

Historical Musicology: Sources, Methods, Interpretations
Edited by Stephen A. Crist and Roberta Montemorra Marvin

The Pleasure of Modernist Music: Listening, Meaning, Intention, Ideology
Edited by Arved Ashby

Debussy's Letters to Inghelbrecht: The Story of a Musical Friendship
Annotated by Margaret G. Cobb

Explaining Tonality: Schenkerian Theory and Beyond
Matthew Brown

The Substance of Things Heard: Writings about Music
Paul Griffiths

Musical Encounters at the 1889 Paris World's Fair
Annegret Fauser

Aspects of Unity in J. S. Bach's Partitas and Suites: An Analytical Study
David W. Beach

Aspects of Unity in J. S. Bach's Partitas and Suites

An Analytical Study

David W. Beach

UNIVERSITY OF ROCHESTER PRESS

First published 2005

University of Rochester Press
668 Mt. Hope Avenue, Rochester, NY 14620, USA
www.urpress.com
and of Boydell & Brewer Limited
PO Box 9, Woodbridge, Suffolk IP12 3DF, UK
www.boydellandbrewer.com

ISBN: 1–58046–202–2

Library of Congress Cataloging-in-Publication Data

Beach, David W., 1933-
Aspects of unity in J.S. Bach's partitas and suites : an analytical study / David W. Beach.
p. cm. – (Eastman studies in music, ISSN 1071-9989 ; v. 33)
Includes bibliographical references and index.
ISBN 1-58046-202-2 (hardcover : alk. paper)
1. Bach, Johann Sebastian, 1685-1750. Suites. 2. Suite (Music) I. Title. II. Series.
MT145.B14B44 2005
784.18′54–dc22

2005020429

A catalogue record for this title is available from the British Library.

This publication is printed on acid-free paper.
Printed in Canada.

to

Marcia Francesca, Juliana, and Matthew

Contents

	List of Figures	viii
	List of Tables	x
	Preface	xi
	The Partitas and Suites of Johann Sebastian Bach	xv

Part I

1	Introduction	3
	The Role of Repetition and Variation	3
	The Variation Suite	8
2	Harmonic Plans	15
3	Motivic Parallels	27
4	Structural Associations	39

Part II

5	Keyboard Suite in A Minor (BWV 818a)	57
6	French Suite VI in E Major (BWV 817)	71
	Epilogue	85
	Appendix: Theoretical Terms and Definitions	87
	Bibliography	89
	Index	91

Figures

1.1. Partita VI (BWV 830) 4
1.2. French Suite II (BWV 813) 5
1.3. French Suite II (BWV 813) 6
1.4. Keyboard Suite in A Minor (BWV 818) 6
1.5. English Suite VI (BWV 811) 7
1.6. Violin Partita I (BWV 1002) 7
1.7. Reincken, *Hortus Musicus*, Sonata I 9
1.8. Reincken, *Hortus Musicus*, Sonata I 10
1.9. Reincken, *Hortus Musicus*, Sonata I 10
1.10. *Praeludium et Partita del tuono terzo* (BWV 833) 11
1.11. Hypothetical model 12

2.1. Partita II (BWV 826) 15
2.2. Partita II (BWV 826) 17
2.3. Partita I (BWV 825) 18
2.4. Partita I (BWV 825) 19
2.5. Partita I (BWV 825) 20
2.6. Partita I (BWV 825) 20
2.7. Partita V (BWV 829) 20
2.8. Partita V (BWV 829) 20
2.9. Partita V (BWV 829) 21
2.10. Cello Suite III (BWV 1009) 21
2.11. Cello Suite III (BWV 1009) 22
2.12. Cello Suite III (BWV 1009) 22
2.13. English Suite V (BWV 810) 23

3.1. Partita III (BWV 827) 28
3.2. English Suite I (BWV 806) 28
3.3. English Suite I (BWV 806) 29
3.4. Partita II (BWV 826) 30
3.5. Keyboard Suite (BWV 821) 30
3.6. Keyboard Suite (BWV 820) 31
3.7. Keyboard Suite (BWV 820) 31
3.8. Orchestral Suite I (BWV 1066) 31
3.9. Keyboard Suite (BWV 822) 32
3.10. Cello Suite I (BWV 1007) 33
3.11. Partita IV (BWV 828) 34
3.12. Partita IV (BWV 828) 35
3.13. Cello Suite IV (BWV 1010) 36
3.14. Cello Suite IV (BWV 1010) 36
3.15. Cello Suite IV (BWV 1010) 36
3.16. Orchestral Suite I (BWV 1066) 37

4.1. Flute Partita (BWV 1013) 39
4.2. Flute Partita (BWV 1013) 40
4.3. Overture in the French Style (BWV 831) 41
4.4. Violin Partita I (BWV 1002) 44
4.5. Violin Partita I (BWV 1002) 46
4.6. Violin Partita II (BWV 1004) 47
4.7. Violin Partita II (BWV 1004) 50
4.8. Violin Partita II (BWV 1004) 51
4.9. Violin Partita II (BWV 1004) 52

5.1. Keyboard Suite in A Minor (BWV 818a) 57
5.2. Interpretation of figure 5.1 58
5.3. Structural models 59
5.4. Prelude 60
5.5. Allemande 61
5.6. Allemande 62
5.7. Courante 63
5.8. Courante 63
5.9. Sarabande 64
5.10. Sarabande simple (BWV 818) 65
5.11. Menuet 66

5.12. Gigue 67
5.13. Gigue 68
5.14. Comparison of structures 69

6.1. Prelude in E (BWV 854/1) 72
6.2. Prelude in E (BWV 854/1) 73
6.3. French Suite in E Major (BWV 817), Allemande 75
6.4. Allemande 75
6.5. Courante 76
6.6. Courante 76
6.7. Sarabande 78
6.8. Gigue 79
6.9. Gavotte 80
6.10. Polonaise 81
6.11. Petit Menuet 82
6.12. Bourrée 83

Tables

1.1 Formal-tonal design of the Praeambulum, Partita V (BWV 829) 3

1.2 Formal-motivic-harmonic design of the Menuet from French Suite II (BWV 813) 5

2.1 Occurrences of ♭7 (A♭) in Partita I (BWV 825) 16

3.1 Harmonization of the stepwise descent from a^2 to $g\sharp^1$ in bars 1–5 of the Allemande of English Suite I (BWV 806) 29

Preface

THIS STUDY IS AN examination of the types and degree of unity—by which I mean the common features—within the individual partitas and suites of Johann Sebastian Bach.[1] While this topic has been touched on in passing in recent publications,[2] it has yet to be examined in depth from an analytical-theoretical perspective. That is the focus and purpose of this investigation.

Perhaps the best way to clarify the focus of this study and how it differs from others of Bach's suites—that is, to clarify what it is as well as what it is not about—is to begin with the term "unity." At a very basic level, unity implies consistency of style, which in this context means consistency of melodic writing (including ornamentation), harmonic language, contrapuntal complexity, texture, dimension, etc. Indeed, changes in these parameters are what differentiate Bach's early style from his more mature works and, for that matter, Bach's styles from those of his contemporaries, a matter of some importance to scholars faced with the difficult task of establishing chronology and authenticity.[3]

Equally important as background to our investigation is a consideration of the circumstances under which the suites were written and first published, matters that have been dealt with in depth by Christoph Wolff and others.[4] As we approach the issue of unity, it would be comforting to know, for example, that Bach conceived of these works as inseparable entities, but alas that is not always the case. As noted by David Schulenberg:

> We know from the successive versions of Bach's later suites that movements could be added or subtracted from such works. Thus, his suites are not closed cycles, but open sets of pieces in the same key . . . . Especially in his early years, Bach, in composing harpsichord pieces, may have set out not to write suites but individual movements that could be grouped together at a later date. . . .[5]

The manner in which some of the suites were altered from early conception to final version raises at least two pertinent questions regarding unity. First, does this suggest we are looking for something that simply isn't there? The evidence, the music, clearly indicates the contrary. Furthermore, it is clear that Bach, and no doubt his predecessors and contemporaries, were well aware of the practice of relating two or more movements of a suite by some unifying device, either a *cantus firmus*, a common harmonic plan, or a motive. Second, knowing the disparate circumstances under which the suites were written and assembled, would it be reasonable to exchange a movement here and there between two suites in the same key without disturbing the sense of unity? There is no simple answer to this question. Perhaps it would work, but only as long as the two were stylistically compatible as defined above.

Let us return now to the matter of focus. I have purposely raised issues of stylistic consistency and historical context, since I believe they are crucial to a comprehensive study of the suites. But I also believe they have been dealt with sufficiently elsewhere, and thus I feel comfortable in looking beyond these matters to other factors—motivic repetition and parallelisms, repeated harmonic and/or voice-leading patterns—that contribute to unity in Bach's suites. In taking this approach, it must be made perfectly clear from the outset that this investigation is not based on any preconceived notions regarding coherence or unity. Rather it reveals and, where possible, attempts to explain the compositional logic of the common elements where they exist, or, more appropriately, where I have perceived them to be. It should come as no surprise to those who are acquainted with these works that analysis reveals a great variety in the degree and types of common elements between or among the movements of a given suite. At one end of the spectrum are those that exhibit a high degree of unity, sometimes readily perceived but other times existing only in the underlying structure, and at the other end are those revealing no such associations. Finally, I want to stress that by focusing on matters of commonality I am not in any way denying the significance of contrast and differentiation between successive movements. These are obvious features of the baroque suite, in most cases derived from the difference dance types of the period. But these features, and for that matter the circumstances mentioned above regarding the progression from early conception to final version of the suites, in no way suggest a lack of continuity or commonality.

According to recent research, Bach is credited with forty-four suites: thirty for keyboard/lute; three for solo violin, six for solo cello, one for solo flute, and four for orchestra. A listing is provided in the chart following this preface. As noted above, the results of my study indicate a great variety in the types and degree of interconnectedness among the movements of the individual suites, ranging from no discernible commonality except consistency of style and dimension, to a few that exhibit considerable and varied associations, sometimes between pairs of movements but in other cases involving several of them. Thus I will not be discussing all forty-four, but only those where I have observed connections, namely in about two-thirds of them. Because I have relied on my ear to tell me where I should dig further, it may be that I have missed some interesting connections. In fact I would be surprised if that were not the case, and thus I have no illusions about this study constituting a definitive statement on unity in these works. Rather this is a beginning, a report on my observations on the types of associations I have found. Some of the works will be discussed only briefly, others in great detail.

Some of Bach's suites, particularly those for solo cello and violin and the three keyboard collections, are generally regarded among the great instrumental works of the mature baroque, the culmination of a tradition in Germany that can be traced through preceding generations—individuals like Kuhnau, Buxtehude, Reincken, Böhm, and others—to Froberger. Since these works come from that tradition, it seems logical that at least some of what I have discovered about Bach's works would apply to the suites by his predecessors and contemporaries like Handel. At the same time, it is clear that Bach surpassed these individuals in the complexity and sophistication of his contrapuntal writing, and thus it would not be surprising to find a richer and more varied complex of relationships in this music.

Aspects of Unity in J. S. Bach's Partitas and Suites is organized as follows. Part I, divided into four chapters, presents the basic findings of this investigation. Chapter 1 is introductory, opening with a discussion of the role of repetition and variation in individual suite movements as preparation for a consideration of inter-movement connections. This is followed by a section dealing with the variation suite, a topic of central importance to this study. Growing out of our discussion of the *Praeludium et Partita del tuono terzo* (BWV 833) at the close of the first chapter, the second opens with two further examples—in this instance, excerpts, not complete movements—where the unifying element is the harmonic succession (common figured-bass pattern) and then presents several examples where the unifying pattern is the overall harmonic scheme rather than the detailed progression of harmonics. While an examination of harmonic progression and large-scale harmonic schemes does indeed reveal a number of interesting connections, this approach, in isolation, leads to only a partial picture of unity in these works. We must also consider motive and voice-leading at various levels. This is the focus of the next two chapters, which form the core of my thesis. Chapter 3 introduces an expanded concept of motive, differentiating among three types: 1) the rhythmic motive; 2) the pitch motive; and 3) the voice-leading motive. Drawing on the latter of these types, chapter 4 deals with voice-leading motives at deeper structural levels. Since harmony, motive, and voice-leading structures are musically dependent, it is inevitable that a focus on one will involve reference to the others. As a result, you will encounter a certain amount of crossing of the topic boundaries as outlined above in the initial chapters. Where all this is intentionally brought together is in Part II, which presents two summary examples: the Keyboard Suite in A Minor (BWV 818a) and French Suite VI in E Major (BWV 817).

I will employ a number of analytic symbols and techniques, whatever seems to convey the idea most clearly. These will include figured bass, harmonic analysis (roman numerals), simple reductions to show underlying voice-leading in the immediate context, and Schenkerian graphs. I have purposely progressed from simple to complex, and I have attempted to make the Schenkerian graphs, which are useful to represent deeper-level musical connections, as clear and accessible as possible.[6] For those not acquainted with this approach I have provided, in an appendix, definitions of theoretical terms employed throughout. It is my hope in writing this book to communicate with all musicians who are interested in these wonderful works and, along the way, to open a path to further research into Bach's music.

In closing I would like to thank a number of individuals for their help and expertise in bringing this project to completion: Jessica Lovett, a former graduate student in musicology at the University of Toronto, and my wife, Marcia, for typing and proofreading various versions of the manuscript; several individuals at University of Rochester Press, including Ralph P. Locke, senior editor of the Eastman Studies in Music series, Timothy Madigan and Suzanne Guiod, former and current editorial directors, respectively, Sue Smith, production manager, and Louise Goldberg, copyeditor; and Dejan Badnjar of Musette Desktop Publishing for his very beautiful settings of the numerous musical examples and particularly the graphs that are so central to this study. I also gratefully acknowledge assistance from the Otto Kinkeldey Publication Endowment Fund of the American Musicological Society.

David Beach
Toronto
July 2004

Notes

1. Bach used various terms to designate a set of dance movements, with or without prelude: Overture, Partita, and Suite. The term *partita* (pl. *partite*) was used by Bach both in its earlier meaning as variation, as in the *Partite diverse*, BWV 766–768, and in its later meaning as a collection of dance movements in the same key. Throughout this work I will use only the word "suite," except where referring to a specific work of different title.

2. The issue of unity in Bach's suites is raised by David Fuller in the article "Suite" in the *New Grove Dictionary of Music and Musicians*, 2nd ed. (New York: Grove, 2001), 24:665–84, and by Hermann Beck in *The Suite*, trans. Robert Kolben (Cologne: Arno Volk, 1966). The most comprehensive view of Bach's compositional style in relation to his suites can be found in the following works by David Schulenberg: "Composition as Variation: Inquiries into the Compositional Procedures of the Bach Circle of Composers," *Current Musicology* 33 (1982): 57–87; *The Keyboard Music of J. S. Bach* (New York: Schirmer, 1992); and "Composition and Improvisation in the School of J. S. Bach," *Bach Perspectives* 1, ed. Russell Stinson (1995): 1–42.

3. Regarding the matter of authorship, it is interesting to note that some works previously attributed to Bach have been identified through efforts of modern scholarship as not authentic. See, for example, the list of doubtful and spurious works for keyboard—including individual dance movements and the Suite in A, BWV 824—compiled by Elwood Derr and listed at the end of section III: 7 (Johann Sebastian Bach) in the Bach entry, *New Grove Dictionary of Music and Musicians*, 2nd ed. (New York: Grove, 2001), 2:372–73.

4. For information specific to the suites, see Schulenberg, The *Keyboard Music of J. S. Bach*. For general information about Bach and his works, see the entry on Johann Sebastian Bach by Christoph Wolff and others in the *New Grove Dictionary of Music and Musicians*, 2nd ed. (New York: Grove, 2001), 2:309–82; and Christoph Wolff, *Johann Sebastian Bach: The Learned Musician* (New York: W. W. Norton, 2000).

5. Schulenberg, *The Keyboard Music of J. S. Bach*, 30.

6. These Schenkerian graphs are of two types: 1) those showing considerable detail (with bar lines included); and 2) those showing only deeper-level connections.

The Partitas and Suites of Johann Sebastian Bach

I. Keyboard/Lute

A. Individual Works

BWV	818/818a	Suite, A Minor
	819	Suite, E-flat Major
	820	Overture, F Major
	821	Suite, B-flat Major
	822	Suite, G Minor
	823	Suite, F Minor
	831	*Overture nach französischer Art, B Minor*
	832	Suite, A Major
	833	*Praeludium et Partita del tuono terzo, F Major*

B. English Suites

BWV	806	Suite, A Major
	807	Suite, A Minor
	808	Suite, G Minor
	809	Suite, F Major
	810	Suite, E Minor
	811	Suite, D Minor

C. French Suites

BWV	812	Suite, D Minor
	813	Suite, C Minor
	814	Suite, B Minor
	815	Suite, E-flat Major
	816	Suite, G Major
	817	Suite, E Major

D. Partitas

BWV	825	Partita, B-flat Major
	826	Partita, C Minor
	827	Partita, A Minor
	828	Partita, D Major
	829	Partita, G Major
	830	Partita, E Minor

E. Lute

BWV	995	Suite, G Minor
	996	Suite, E Minor
	997	Partita, C Minor

II. Other Solo Instruments

A. Violin

BWV	1002	Partita, B Minor
	1004	Partita, D Minor
	1006	Partita, E Major

B. Cello

BWV	1007	Suite, G Major
	1008	Suite, D Minor
	1009	Suite, C Major
	1010	Suite, E-flat Major
	1011	Suite, C Minor
	1012	Suite, D Major

C. Flute

BWV	1013	Partita, A Minor

III. Orchestra

BWV	1066	Suite, C Major
	1067	Suite, B Minor
	1068	Suite, D Major
	1069	Suite, D Major

Part I

1

Introduction

The Role of Repetition and Variation

A LOGICAL POINT OF DEPARTURE for a study of unity in Bach's suites is an examination of the role played by repetition and variation, first within individual movements and then between or among them. Repetition—of a harmonic pattern, a motive, or a theme—is basic to our perception of form in this music; without it there is no form or coherence. The important role of motivic repetition in Bach's suites, which is the primary focus of chapters 3 and 4, was indelibly stamped on my consciousness many years ago by the following experiment. One of my professors announced to his class on Form that he wanted us to listen to a short composition he was going to perform on the piano, and to identify what, if anything, might be lacking in it. He proceeded to play what we all assumed was a suite movement by Bach, an Allemande, as I recall. Actually, what he played was a hybrid formed by juxtaposing the first part of one Allemande with the second part of another one in the same key. At first I listened for harmonic anomalies, but of course there were none; the piece progressed normally. It was only with subsequent hearings that the "problem" became apparent. The two parts were not compositionally linked in any way. That is, the hybrid movement was lacking in motivic integrity. We shall return to this point later on.

The role of motive in defining form is most clearly evident in some of the introductory movements of the suites, the preludes and overtures.[1] Consider, for example, the Praeambulum from Partita V (BWV 829), where the form is defined by repetitions of a single idea, a motive, at different tonal levels. Statements of this one idea are connected by passages consisting of scales, arpeggios, and sequences. A diagram outlining the main formal divisions and the corresponding tonal progression of this simple movement is provided in table 1.1.

Another clear example of the role of motive in defining the form is the opening movement, the Toccata, from Partita VI (BWV 830). The form of the movement is ternary: A (1–26)–B (27–89)–A^1 (89–108). The A section, which is improvisatory and chromatic in character, sets the tone for much of the partita. The improvisatory character is evident in the Allemanda and Sarabande, and the chromaticism becomes dominant in the Corrente and Gigue, less so in the Sarabande. The A section is harmonically closed (E minor), alternating between statements of the main idea (see figure 1.1a), characterized by the dotted rhythmic figure and following appoggiatura (the "sighing" motive), and repeated equal-note figures. The dotted rhythm of the main idea reappears in the Allemanda, Sarabande, and Gigue. The B section is a 3-part fugue. Though clearly a contrasting section in terms of character and texture, the fugue subject may be understood as derived from the opening idea. Here the approach to the main tone (g) occurs by stepwise ascent, each step being articulated by the sighing motive and further elaborated by mordents, rather than arpeggiation as in the opening dramatic gesture. In addition, prolongation of the main tone by its upper neighbor, evident in the opening two bars, is also represented here, though in this instance the tone a passes through the following g on its way to scale degree 2 (f♯) and on to local closure, as shown in the underlying voice-leading

Table 1.1. Formal-tonal design of the Praeambulum, Partita V (BWV 829)

Bars	Content	Tonal Level
1–4	motive	I
5–16	scale passages and arpeggios leading to	
17–20	motive	V
21–40	sequential passages, arpeggios leading to	
41–44	motive	VI
45–64	scale passage and sequences leading to	
65–68	motive	IV
69–72	sequence leading to	
73–87	prolongation of the dominant (This passage introduces the chromatic elements b♭ (♭3) and e♭ (♭6), both of which appear in the Allemande.)	V
88–95	extension of the tonic (Note the registrally expanded octave descent from g^2.)	I

Note. The registers of pitch are designated throughout this work by the system whereby middle c is c^1. Thus g^2 is the g an octave and a fifth above middle c.

Figure 1.1. Partita VI (BWV 830), Toccata

superimposed on the music in figure 1.1b.[2] The final section returns to the improvisatory character of the opening, beginning in B minor (V) and ending in the tonic.

These are but two of the simpler examples of an interesting body of works, the preludes, that are worthy of further study—not only the form-defining role of motive but also the links to the suite movements that follow.

Let us return now to the matter alluded to in the opening paragraph, namely the important role of repetition, particularly varied repetition, in the binary dance movements, where, with few exceptions, we find the opening material restated in varied form at the beginning of the second part. In all such cases the original material is transposed, either to the dominant or to the relative major, and in some instances, particularly in gigues, the original idea appears inverted as well. Rarely is the transposition an exact replica. More frequently it is transformed in some way, yet with a recognizable link, perhaps in some instances only rhythmic, to the opening material. In those few instances where there is no reference to the opening material after the double bar there is a link to the preceding material at the cadence, creating a sense of continuity. In all these instances, the repetition and/or link contribute significantly to the aural logic and compositional integrity of the work.

There are a few movements where we find a return to the opening material at the original pitch level in addition to the transposed (and sometimes inverted) reference immediately following the repeat of part 1. Two movements, the Sarabande and Bourrée anglaise from the flute partita (BWV 1013), are in rounded binary form, where the repetition of the opening material occurs in conjunction with a return to the tonic, a procedure that becomes the standard in classical composition. The same procedure is followed in the Courante of the first orchestral suite (BWV 1066). In at least three other movements we find a variant of this procedure, namely where the repetition at the original pitch level does not occur with a true return to the tonic. Consider, for example, the Polonaise and Menuet from French Suite VI (BWV 817). The return at bar 17 in the former movement might at first appear to be a double return, but in this case the E-major harmony is not tonic, but V of the subdominant. And the return at bars 17–18 of the latter is subsumed under a prolongation of the dominant arrived at in the preceding bar. The Sarabande from French Suite V (BWV 816) presents yet a different situation. Here the brief reference to the opening at bar 25 is reharmonized (vi).

The Menuet from French Suite II (BWV 813) provides an excellent summary example to our brief examination of the roles of motivic repetition within a single movement and a glimpse ahead to the types of relationships discussed in chapters three and four. The complete score of this movement is reproduced in figure 1.2, and on the score I have indicated repetitions of two surface motives: a, first stated in the right-hand part in bar 1, by a straight bracket; and b, first stated in the right-hand part in bar 5, by a curly bracket. These two ideas are closely related; what differentiates them are their contours. Examination of their deployment reveals how cleverly Bach has used them to articulate the phrase structure. Consider, for example, the first part of the binary form, a modulating period that is divided into two four-bar phrases. Motive a initiates phrase 1, and b initiates phrase 2. Looking now to the next eight-bar period we see that the same pattern applies. This is followed by an eight-bar sequence derived from motive b that connects the subdominant, the goal of the preceding period, to the dominant in bar 24. At this point we might expect a return to the tonic and a final eight-bar period closing the movement. Indeed there are eight bars following, the first four initiated by motive a and the last four by motive b, by now a familiar scheme. But instead of a return to the tonic in conjunction with the return of motive a, Bach extends the dominant for four bars, with motive a now in the

Figure 1.2. French Suite II (BWV 813), Menuet

left-hand part, and the return to the tonic is delayed until bar 29, coinciding with the final appearance of motive b. A diagram of the formal divisions labeled according to motivic articulation and the accompanying harmonic scheme of this movement is provided in table 1.2.

Table 1.2. Formal – Motivic – Harmonic Design of the MENUET from French Suite II (BWV 813)

8	8	8	8
a (4) + b (4)	a (4) + b (4)	sequence (b)	a (4) + b (4)
i←V, i [V] III	III←V, [V] iv	················· V	———— i ii V i

Careful examination of this movement reveals that there is yet another motivic idea that plays an important role in this movement. It is the third a♭–g–f, first stated in the right-hand part in bar 2. I have circled its repetitions on the score (figure 1.2) and also indicated its prominent placement at the cadence in bars 15–16. It is important for us to view the original statement of this idea in its larger context. As shown at a in figure 1.3, a sketch of the voice-leading of bars 1–5, the $a\flat^2$–g^2–f^2 continues on to $e\flat^2$ on the downbeat of bar 3, moving in parallel tenths with the bass. The motion continues on to d^2 and from there descends rapidly, eventually reaching the inner voice tone g^1. If we now look at the underlying voice-leading of the passage beginning in bar 17, we see that it is far more than a sequence based on motive b. It is a clever expansion of bars 2–4. Here the motion in parallel tenths, which was elaborated by a varied repetition of motive a in the left-hand part of bar 2 (see figure 1.2), is expanded by a 10–7 sequence. That is, what had occupied one measure (bar 2) has been expanded to six. Any doubt about this reference should be erased by the continuation. Bars 23–24 are an almost exact replica of bars 3–4. This time the melodic line does not return to $e\flat^2$ over tonic harmony, as it had in bar 5, but the line is transferred to the bass, now articulated by statements of motive a, as part of the extended dominant harmony.

A natural starting point for an investigation of Bach's variation technique exists in those suite movements with Doubles, where one can observe an additional stage of elaboration of an underlying voice-leading pattern.[3] Consider, for example, the opening four bars of the Sarabande and its variation from the Keyboard Suite in A Minor, BWV 818, which are provided in figure 1.4, along with a reduction of the voice-leading.[4] A salient feature of the Sarabande simple is the figure first stated in the right-hand part in bar 1, a slightly embellished

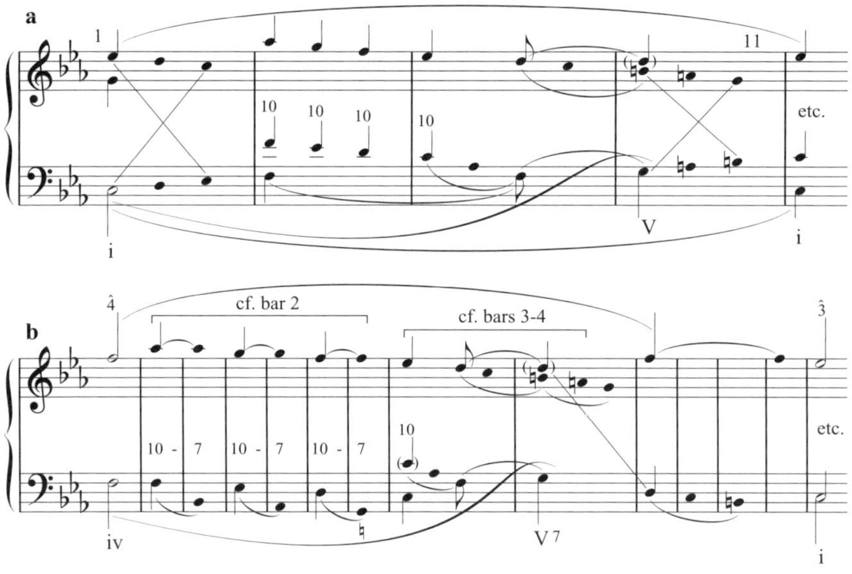

Figure 1.3. French Suite II (BWV 813), Menuet. Comparison of bars 2–4 and 17–28

arpeggiation of the tonic triad downward from e^2, repeated a step lower in bar 2, and then varied in bar 3 leading to the dominant (bar 4). Notice that Bach preserves this manner of varied repetition in the Double, though here the arpeggiation is filled in by passing tones and the inner and outer voices are connected by arpeggiation on the third beat. Bach also maintains the elaboration of the fifth of the triad by its upper neighbor, f^2, in the variation.

A second example, the opening of the Sarabande from English Suite VI (BWV 811) and the corresponding bars from its Double, is provided in figure 1.5. Here the Sarabande is very simple, almost identical to the underlying voice-leading shown, except for repeated notes and embellishments. The Double moves in steady eighth-note motion that articulates the inner voices by means of elaborated arpeggiation, where chord tones are introduced by step from below. The top part is elaborated only minimally by arpeggiation (thirds above) and by passing motion.

Figure 1.4. Keyboard Suite in A Minor (BWV 818)

Figure 1.6a provides the opening of the Allemanda from the first violin partita (BWV 1002), the corresponding bars of the Double, and above a reduction of the Allemanda. Figures 1.6b, 1.6c, and 1.6d provide the same for the Sarabande, Tempo di Borea, and Corrente, respectively. The reason for this organization, that is, of placing the Corrente last, is to highlight the motivic similarity among the other three movements, a matter to be discussed in greater detail later on. In each of these three movements the main melodic tone, f♯², is first prolonged by its upper neighbor note before descending to the local goal. In both the Allemanda and Tempo di Borea, the f♯² is temporarily covered by b^2,

Figure 1.5. English Suite VI (BWV 811)

Figure 1.6. Violin Partita I (BWV 1002)

strengthening the association. By contrast, the reduction of the corrente (figure 1.6d) shows that its opening melodic gesture is an ascending line. Returning now to the matter at hand, we can see that the Double of the Allemanda does not preserve the rhythmic character of the original, but rather progresses by sixteenth notes. The individual lines are articulated through arpeggiation and passing notes, and the bass line begins an octave higher. The same general procedure is followed in the Doubles of the Sarabande and Tempo di Borea.[5] By contrast, the arpeggiation figuration of the Corrente is transformed into scale passages—filled-in arpeggiations—in its Double.

Figure 1.6. (continued)

Though the sample is relatively small here, there are at least two general principles that can be drawn from examining all thirteen movements with their Doubles.[6] First, it seems that many of the variation movements employ a consistent note value, the eighth or the sixteenth. In these instances the rhythmic character of the original movement is lost; what is being varied in each case is the underlying voice-leading. We have just seen three very clear examples of this procedure in the Allemanda–Double, Sarabande–Double, and Tempo di Borea–Double of the first violin partita. This is also true in the Double of the Sarabande from the sixth English Suite and the Double of the Gigue from the third lute suite (BWV 997). By contrast, there are several examples where the rhythmic character of the original is retained, as in the two Doubles of Courante II from English Suite I (BWV 806), the two Sarabandes with *agréments* from English Suites II and III (BWV 807 and 808), and the Sarabande double from the Keyboard Suite BWV 818. In the first of these, the original character of the Courante is retained in the right-hand part. The left-hand part of the first variation maintains continuous eighth-note motion, but this is not followed in the second Double. And, as we have observed in figure 1.4, the repeated pattern of the Sarabande simple from BWV 818 is not lost, but rather replaced by a variant in its Double. Second, one can take as a general principle that sustained chords in the original movement are replaced by arpeggiated chords in the variation and that arpeggiated chords in the original are filled in by passing notes. The procedure can be observed in the examples presented in figures 1.4 through 1.6.[7]

The Variation Suite

Unity in the baroque suite is most clearly represented in what is appropriately called the variation suite, a generic term encompassing a variety of practices. On the one hand, we have examples like Buxtehude's famous suite *Auf meinen lieben Gott* (BuxWV 179), where each of the movements—the chorale setting followed by a Double, then a Sarabande, Courante, and Gigue—are clear variations of the opening chorale, both melody and bass.[8] (This type of variation set is represented in Bach's work by his chorale variations, BWV 766–768, with the obvious difference that the "partite" are not cast as dance movements.) The composing of such a suite, where all movements are derived from a single source (in this case a figured bass rather than a chorale setting), is the goal of the *Handleitung zur Variation* (1706), Part II of the *Musicalische Handleitung,* by Friederich Erhard Niedt.[9] It is significant that Niedt begins instruction with the study of thoroughbass in Part I of his treatise before progressing to the study of variations and the application of variation technique in Part II. This second part begins in the tradition of the older diminution treatises with a listing of the many ways to vary each diatonic interval, from unison to octave, both ascending and descending, following which this knowledge is applied to a simple bass recast in different meters. The following chapter then adds the right hand above this same bass and presents different ways to vary this part—by means of simple arpeggiation, running passages, and repeated patterns. Having added the right-hand part, Niedt then proceeds to demonstrate how to vary the common signatures of figured bass, those introduced in the first part of the treatise, and he then applies this knowledge to a given figured bass. Where all this is leading is to the composition of a series of suite movements based on the given bass, which is subsequently rewritten in various meters to fit the character of the different dance types. The results are not always satisfying musically, but this does not lessen the historical significance of this unique work.

There is a fair amount of circumstantial evidence connecting Niedt to Bach. We do know, for example, that Niedt's teacher, the one referred to in the preface to Part I of *Die musicalische Handleitung,* was Johann Nicolaus

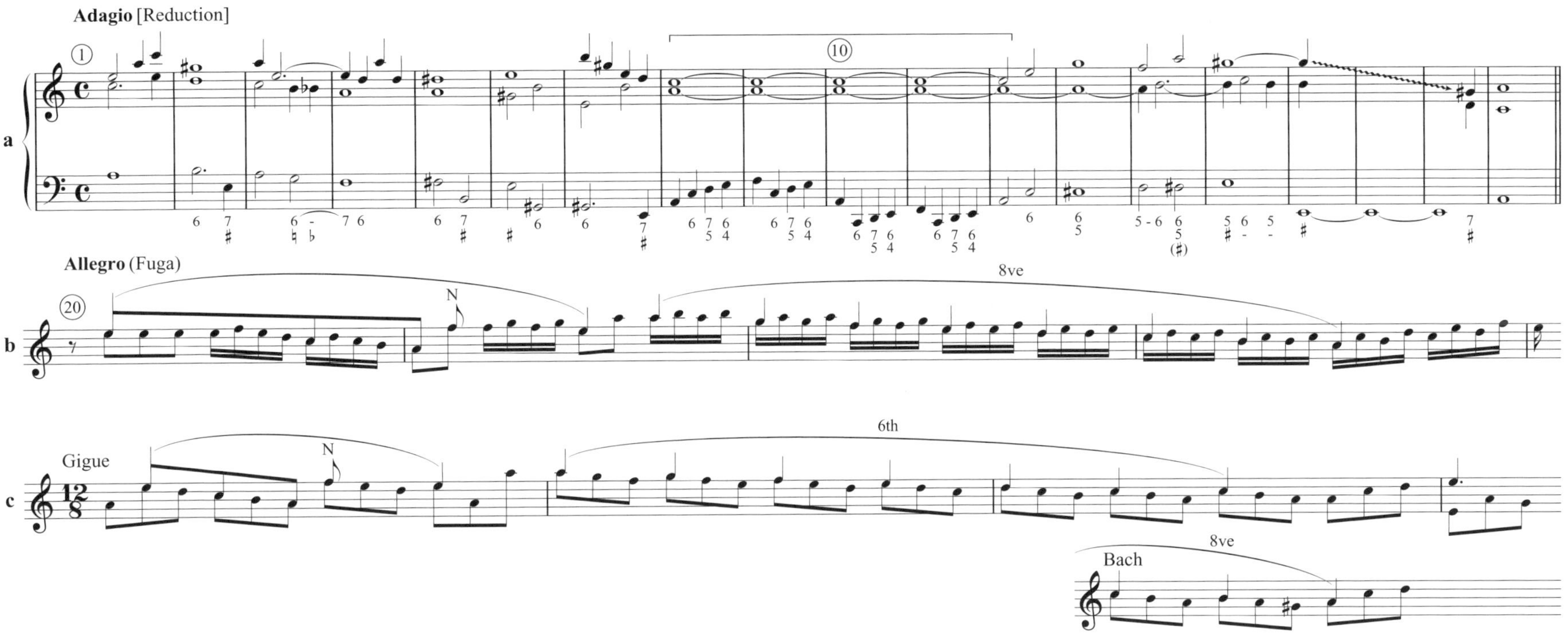

Figure 1.7. Reincken, *Hortus Musicus*, Sonata I

Bach (1669–1753), Johann Sebastian's cousin. As reported by David Schulenberg, this fact has led to speculation that Niedt's treatise may well outline what was a Bach family tradition in composition.[10] As we have already noted, Niedt does begin instruction with thorough-bass realization in four parts, which according to both Carl Philipp Emanuel and his father's student, Johann Philipp Kirnberger, was exactly what Johann Sebastian did in the instruction of his students.[11] A further piece of evidence comes to us in the form of a manuscript consisting of basic instruction and practical exercises in four-part thorough-bass realization, apparently compiled by Bach for his students at the Leipzig Thomasschule.[12] The second part of this manuscript, titled *Gründlicher Unterricht des General-Basses*, is a close paraphrase of the initial volume of the Niedt treatise.[13]

Whether or not Bach was acquainted with volume 2 of the Niedt treatise, the one on variation technique, is an open question, but not crucial as a link between Bach and the tradition of the variation suite. That link is clearly established by Bach's keyboard arrangement (BWV 965) of Sonata I from Johann Adam Reincken's *Hortus Musicus* (1687). Examination of the Reincken sonata reveals that the composer's means of creating associations among the movements are more varied than the single approach outlined by Niedt in his treatise. Two of the movements, the Allemande and the Courante, are indeed derived from the same harmonic/contrapuntal framework, but in other instances the associations are created by motivic references and even direct quotation.

The prelude to the Reincken sonata begins with a slow introductory section (Adagio) followed by an Allegro (*fuga*) and then a third section alternating between slow and fast tempi for solo violin and continuo. A reduction of the opening Adagio is provided in figure 1.7 (level a). Note the bracket above bars 8–12, which highlights a passage that is

Figure 1.8. Reincken, *Hortus Musicus*, Sonata I

stated in varied form in both the Allemande and Courante. This passage is immediately recognizable because of its static quality. Level b presents the fugue subject of the middle section. As shown by the analytical additions, the first part of the subject is characterized first by the descending arpeggiation of the tonic triad followed by the reintroduction of the primary tone (e^2) by its upper neighbor. This is followed by an elaborated statement of the octave descent from a^2 to a^1. The derivation of the Gigue subject (shown at level c) from the fugue subject is obvious. It is curious that Reincken altered the descending octave to a descending sixth, stalling at c^2, and equally interesting that Bach changes this feature in his keyboard arrangement, restoring the octave progression and thus strengthening the motivic correspondence between Fugue and Gigue.

Reductions of the opening measures of the Allemande and Courante are provided in figure 1.8, aligned to show the correspondence between them. It is perfectly clear that the two are based on the same contrapuntal model, that is, on the same melodic *and* harmonic framework.

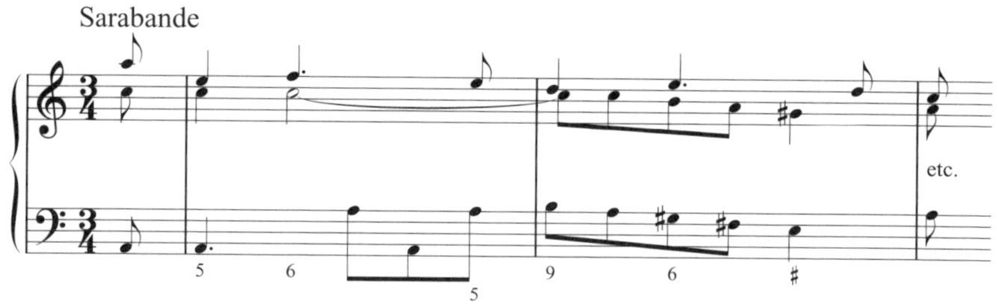

Figure 1.9. Reincken, *Hortus Musicus*, Sonata I

This is a stronger association than one finds in the Niedt treatise, where all movements are based on the same figured bass (bass line and harmonic succession) but not melody. Here the Courante is truly a variation of the Allemande. Furthermore, as noted above, the characteristic static passage from the Adagio is repeated in varied form in both these movements (see brackets), enhancing the sense of continuity from movement to movement. Since the Gigue is derived from the earlier fugue, that leaves only the Sarabande, the opening measures of which are given in figure 1.9. While the movement as a whole cannot be considered a variation of preceding movements, the reference to the melodic contour and pitches of the previous two movements (figure 1.8) is clear in the opening measures.

What might Bach have learned from preparing an elaborate keyboard arrangement of this sonata? Perhaps the greatest lesson to be learned is that there are various ways at creating associations between/among movements, ranging from direct quotation and motivic reference to various levels of derivation, including the recomposition of an entire movement to create something new. It should come as not surprise that we find all this, and even more, in his suites.

So, did Bach write any variation suites? According to both Elaine Sisman and David Schulenberg, there is but a single example among Bach's numerous suites, the early work titled *Praeludium et Partita del tuono terzo* (BWV 833).[14] Perhaps they are correct according to a narrow definition of the term, though, as we shall see, there are several other suites by Bach that exhibit far greater inter-movement associations. The

Figure 1.10. *Praeludium et Partita del tuono terzo* (BWV 833). Comparison of Allemande and Courante

Allemande and Courante movements of this work form a variation pair with two common features that are immediately apparent. First the modal inflection g–a♭–g, that is, scale degrees 5–♭6–5 in the key of the dominant, that appears in bar 7 of the Allemande is restated at the equivalent place in the Courante. And second the repeated note pattern that is pervasive in the Allemande reappears at several points in the Courante. However, what qualifies these two movements as a variation pair is the fact that they are based on the same underlying framework, though not as clearly as we have seen in the Reincken sonata. David Schulenberg has described the relationship as follows:

> The courante is notated in [3/4] . . . but is really in what we would call [6/4] . . . two measures here correspond to one in the allemande. Although the two movements share some motivic material, their main common point is the harmonic ground, a notable feature of which is the use of the minor mode in the closing phrase of the first half. . . . At one point the courante departs from the ground, two bars (29–30) being inserted. But because several other bars of the model are compressed, the length remains the same as in the allemande: twenty bars of [6/4][15]

Schulenberg's explanation reflects the complex and sometimes tentative correspondences between these two movements, as revealed in figure 1.10. Here the two basses are aligned and lines are drawn between the two to indicate equivalent harmonies. The correspondence between the two is clear through bar 10 of the Allemande and again from bar 16 to the end, but less so in the intervening section. The two bars of the Courante described by Schulenberg as being inserted, highlighted in figure 1.10 by a bracket and asterisk, arise from extension of the F-major harmony, here functioning as V of the subdominant, the arrival at which in bar 16 is the point where the two basses once again begin to align. Because the Allemande comes first, it naturally is taken as the model from which the Courante is derived, but perhaps neither should be considered as the source. Instead one might consider both to be elaborations of a much simpler abstract model, as provided in figure 1.11.

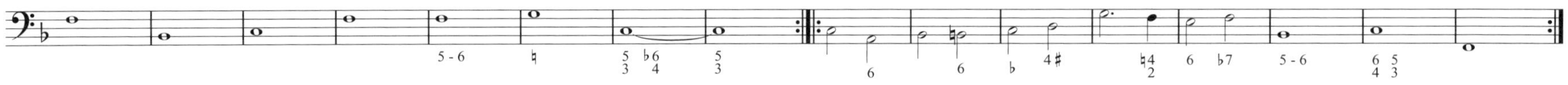

Figure 1.11. Hypothetical model

Notes

1. The introductory movements of Partitas II, III, and VI (BWV 826, 827, and 830) are titled Sinfonia, Fantasia, and Toccata, respectively. All other introductory movements in the suites are titled Prelude (Praeludium, Praeambulum) or Ouverture.

2. My placement of stems showing the stepwise ascent in figure 1.1b may at first appear counterintuitive. That is, why not place them on the accented notes? The reason is the implied harmonic support, which suggests that the accented pitches, emphasized here by ornaments, are appoggiaturas and thus not supported harmonically. This simple example illustrates the potential confusion that can arise in analysis depending on whether one is following the musical articulations or the underlying organization.

3. The following movements from the suites have Doubles:

BWV	Suite	Movements with Doubles
806	English Suite I	Courante II (2 Doubles)
811	English Suite VI	Sarabande
818	Keyboard Suite	Sarabande
833	*Praeludium et Partita del tuono terzo*	Sarabande
997	Lute Suite III	Gigue
1002	Violin Partita I	Allemanda, Corrente, Sarabande, Tempo di Borea
1067	Orchestral Suite II	Polonaise

Also in this category are movements with added embellishments, the Sarabande movements with *agréments* from English Suites II and III (BWV 807 and 808). See also the Chaconne from Violin Partita II (BWV 1004).

4. The type of reduction used here and elsewhere is a simplification of the voice-leading, resulting from the elimination of unessential embellishments (all but metric suspensions) and rhythmic shifts. Note values in the reduction indicate duration of control or influence, in contrast to the sketch, where note values indicate relative structural weight.

5. Notes implied by context but not actually stated in the music are indicated in the reductions (and later in sketches) by parentheses. See, for example, the c$\sharp^2$ in my reduction of the Sarabande (top voice, bar 4) and the implied bass note f$\sharp^1$ on the downbeat of bar 2 of the Tempo di Borea.

6. An anomaly is the Polonaise and its Double from the second orchestral suite (BWV 1067). In this case the Double consists of an elaborate flute obbligato added above the original melodic part. Careful examination of the flute obbligato reveals its origins in the original melody.

7. Bach's Double movements have been discussed only briefly here because the topic of diminution technique is not central to the main thesis of this study. However, they are worthy of more careful examination in themselves and in relation to those of his immediate predecessors and contemporaries, particularly Handel.

8. The Buxtehude, where all subsequent movements are variations of the opening chorale, is an extreme. It is far more common that only two or some of the movements of a variation suite are so related.

9. Friederich Erhard Niedt, *Musicalische Handleitung I: Vom General-Bass* (1700); *II: Handleitung zur Variation* (1706; 2nd expanded edition, ed. J. Mattheson, 1721); *III: Von Contra-Punct, Canon, Motetten, Choral, Recitativ-Stylo, und Cavatten*, ed. J. Mattheson (1717). English translation as *Musical Guide* by Pamela Poulin and Imgard C. Taylor. Oxford: Oxford University Press, 1989.

10. See David Schulenberg, "Composition and Improvisation in the School of J. S. Bach," *Bach Perspectives* 1, ed. Russell Stinson (Lincoln: University of Nebraska Press, 1995), 8n22.

11. C. P. E. Bach provides the following well-known description of his father's method of teaching in a letter to Forkel, dated 13 January 1775 (quoted in *The New Bach Reader*, ed. Hans T. David and Arthur Mendel, rev. and expanded Christoph Wolff [New York: W. W. Norton, 1998]: 399):

> His pupils had to begin their studies by learning pure four-part thoroughbass. From this he went to chorales; first he added the basses to them himself, and they had to invent the alto and tenor. Then he taught them to devise the basses

themselves. He particularly insisted on the writing out of the thoroughbass in [four real] parts. . . . The realization of a thoroughbass and the introduction to chorales are without doubt the best way of studying composition, as far as harmony is concerned.

Kirnberger, who studied with Bach in Leipzig (1739–41), claimed his major work, *Die Kunst des reinen Satzes in der Musik* (I, 1771; II, 1776–79), was based on Bach's method of teaching, a claim supported by Forkel. This work begins with instruction in pure four-part writing, and later in the work—when he begins instruction in simple counterpoint—Kirnberger breaks with tradition by insisting on starting in four parts and only later learning the more difficult task of writing in two and three parts.

12. The manuscript (AA27.224, Bibliothèque du Conservatoire Royal de Musique, Brussels) is titled "Des königlichen Hoff-Compositeurs und Capellmeisters ingleichen Directoris Musices wie auch Cantoris der Thomas-Schule Herrn Johann Sebastian Bach zu Leipzig Vorschriften und Grundsätze zum vierstimmigen Spielen des General-Bass oder Accompaniment für seine Scholaren in der Music, 1738." The title page is in the hand of Carl August Thième, who studied with Bach between 1735 and 1745.

13. Variants from the Niedt treatise are clearly indicated by Pamela Poulin in her translation of this work. See *J. S. Bach's Precepts and Principles for Playing the Thorough-Bass or Accompaniment in Four Parts* (Oxford: Clarendon Press, 1994.)

14. Elaine Sisman, "Variations," *New Grove Dictionary of Music and Musicians*, ed. Stanley Sadie, 2nd ed. (New York: Grove, 2001), 26:284–326; David Schulenberg, "Composition and Improvisation in the School of J. S. Bach," 9.

15. Schulenberg, *The Keyboard Music of J. S. Bach* (New York: Schirmer, 1992), 36.

2

Harmonic Plans

IN THIS CHAPTER we will consider two types of harmonic repetition exhibited in the suites: 1) a succession of chords over several measures common to a pair of movements; and 2) a large-scale harmonic scheme shared by several movements. We have already encountered a prime example of the first type in our brief consideration of the Allemande–Courante pair from the *Praeludium et Partita del tuono terzo* (BWV 833) at the close of the preceding chapter. This appears to be the sole instance throughout the forty-four suites where this type of relationship exists throughout the two movements. However, there are at least two instances where this relationship holds for a significant portion of a movement pair. One of these occurs in the first parts of the Allemande and the Courante from Partita II (BWV 826). Though very different in character and surface design, the two movements share a common plan leading from the tonic to the cadence on the dominant at the close of part 1. (The scores of the Allemande, bars 7–16, and of the Courante, bars 6–12, are provided in figure 2.1, and reductions of these passages are provided in figure 2.2). What is striking to the ear is the exact repetition of harmonies connecting the tonic harmony with the same chord in six-three position (Allemande, bar 9; Courante, bar 8), now functioning as iv^6 in the key of the dominant. (An interpretation of the harmonic succession using roman numerals is provided below the passage from the Courante). From this point the two movements progress differently, though arriving at the same goal. However, both movements contain parenthetical registral digressions, and further scrutiny reveals that both melodic passages are elaborations of the same underlying descent by step from e♭^{2} to g^1.[1]

A similar relationship exists between the opening measures of the Allemande and the Sarabande from Partita I (BWV 825), the scores of which are provided in figure 2.3. As shown in figure 2.4, a comparison of the essential voice-leading of the first parts of these two movements, the relationship is clear through bar 9 of each, the point of initial arrival

Figure 2.1. Partita II (BWV 826)

at the dominant. (It is only in the subsequent measures, namely in the confirmation of the dominant, that the two differ significantly). Both open in a similar fashion, with the motion 8–♭7 over a tonic pedal, and, following the initial four-bar prolongation of the tonic, both progress through the same or equivalent harmonies to the dominant (bar 9). As shown by the roman numerals below the voice-leading reductions, the

Courante, 6-12

Figure 2.1. (continued)

"modulation" to the dominant is accomplished through a common pivot: vi in the original key (B♭) becomes ii in the dominant.[2] This same means of modulating to the dominant has been foreshadowed in the Praeludium (bars 7–14).

In very similar fashion to what we encountered with the first example, the Allemande and Courante from the second partita, the harmonic relationship between this movement pair continues into the second part, at least with respect to larger harmonic goals if not in the detailed succession of harmonies. Both movements contain a confirmed modulation to the supertonic, the Allemande in bar 32 and the Sarabande in bar 20. A comparison of the overall harmonic plan of both movements, utilizing both music notation (an analytic bass line showing the hierarchy of harmonies) and roman numeral representation of harmonic functions, is provided in figure 2.5.[3] Though the correspondence is not exact, it is clear that the underlying harmonic design of both movements is essentially the same. As shown on the lowest system, the fundamental progression of both movements is I . . . ii V I.

Table 2.1. Occurrences of ♭7 (A♭) in Partita I (BWV 825)

Movement	Measure Numbers	Function
Praeludium	7, 14, 19, 20	I♭7 (= V^7 of IV)
Allemande	1	I♭7
	15	$\flat\hat{3}$ of V (F)
	23–26	leading to ii (c)
	33, 35, 36, 38	I♭7
Corrente	16	$\flat\hat{3}$ of V
	37–39	leading to E♭ as VI of ii (c)
	47, 58	I♭7
Sarabande	2	I♭7
	17–18	°7 of ii (c)
	25	I♭7
Menuet I	5, 26	I♭7
	29	$\hat{4}$ in IV (E♭)
Menuet II	2, 13	I♭7
Gigue	10, 12	♭3 of V (F)
	13	°7 of V of V
	18	I♭7

As we look beyond the Allemande–Sarabande pairing, it is of utmost importance to our general topic of unity within the suites to note that every movement in this work is related by virtue of a common element, the flat or lowered seventh degree (a♭) of the B♭-major scale. Its employment is so pervasive and in many cases so blatant, as employed in the opening bars of both the Allemande and Sarabande (see figure 2.3), that it achieves the status of a motive. In most cases, a♭ is employed as ♭7 in B♭, that is, as part of I♭7 (= V^7 of IV), resulting in an emphasis throughout the suite on the subdominant, but it is also employed in relation to other harmonies/temporary key centers as well. A listing of its occurrences and functions in each of the movements is provided in table 2.1.

In summary, we note the following features of the first partita. First, there is a thread—the pervasive a♭—that runs through the entire suite, commencing with the Praeludium. Second, the Allemande and Sarabande are paired by virtue of the similarity in their harmonic plans, both in terms of their overall tonal design and the succession of harmonies, particularly in their first parts. There is yet another point relevant to the topic at hand, namely that the remaining movements,

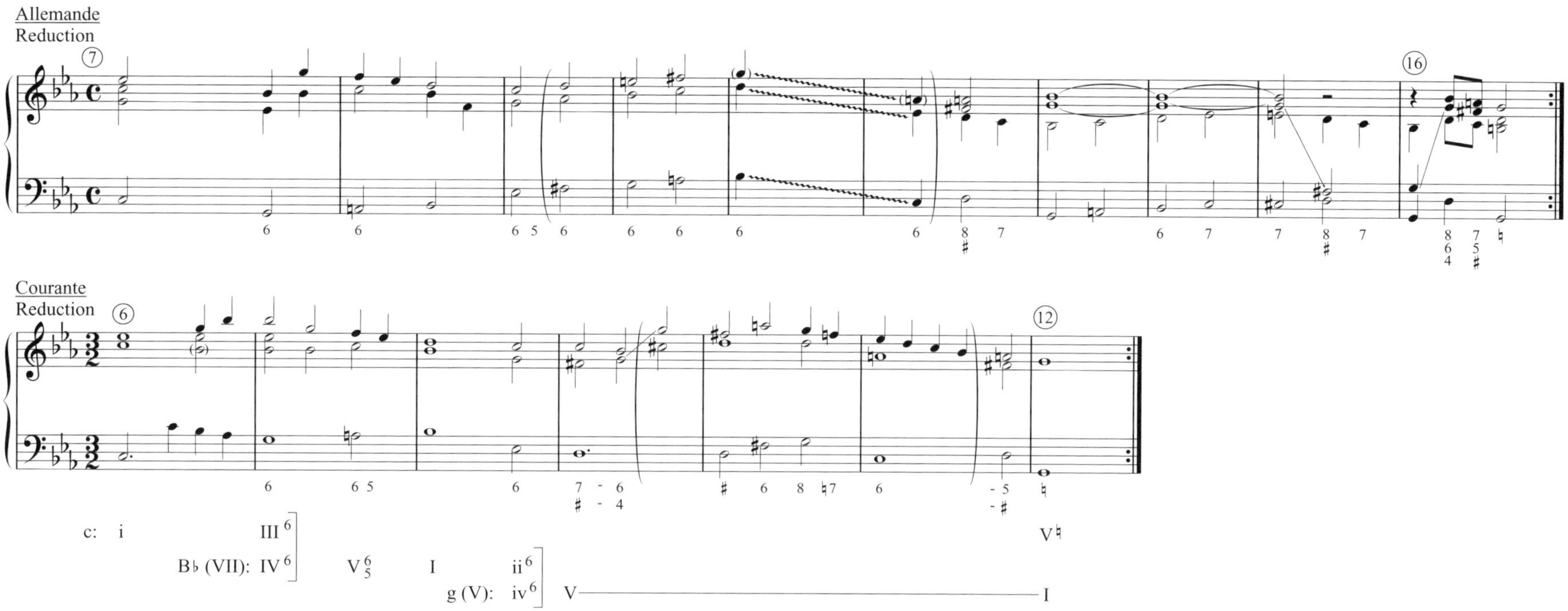

Figure 2.2. Partita II (BWV 826), Comparison of Allemande, mm. 7–16, and Courante, mm. 6–12

excluding the Praeludium, all follow the same large-scale harmonic plan, a different plan from the one that is exhibited in the Allemande and Sarabande. This large-scale tonal design, as it occurs in Menuet II, is shown in figure 2.6. In the other three movements the motion to the submediant (vi) is confirmed by a cadence in that key—at bar 46 in the Corrente, at bar 24 in Menuet I, and at bar 28 in the Giga. In all cases the modulation to vi is followed directly by a secondary dominant (I♭7) leading to the subdominant—at bar 48 in the Corrente, at bar 27 in Menuet I, and at bar 30 in the Giga—thus completing the large-scale descending third progression leading on to the dominant and closure. This point leads us to the second of our topics within this chapter, a consideration of suites containing several movements related by virtue of a common large-scale harmonic design.

Several of the Bach suites are unified by the employment of the same large-scale harmonic design in a number of their movements. One might argue that this is unexceptional, since almost all of the binary dance movements, certainly all those in the major mode, progress to the dominant at the end of part 1 and then close in the tonic at the end of part 2. This is certainly true, but what we are considering here in addition to these basic features is a design incorporating, at the very least, a common modulation, confirmed by a cadence, internal to the second part. There are numerous suites where this does not occur, but when it does, the repetition is apparent to the trained musician; even short of that, it at least contributes to the sense of coherence to the less sophisticated listener.

A clear example of this phenomenon occurs in Partita V (BWV 829). Five of its movements—Allemande, Corrente, Sarabande, Tempo di

Figure 2.3. Partita I (BWV 825), Allemande, part 1, and Sarabande, part 1

Figure 2.3. (continued)

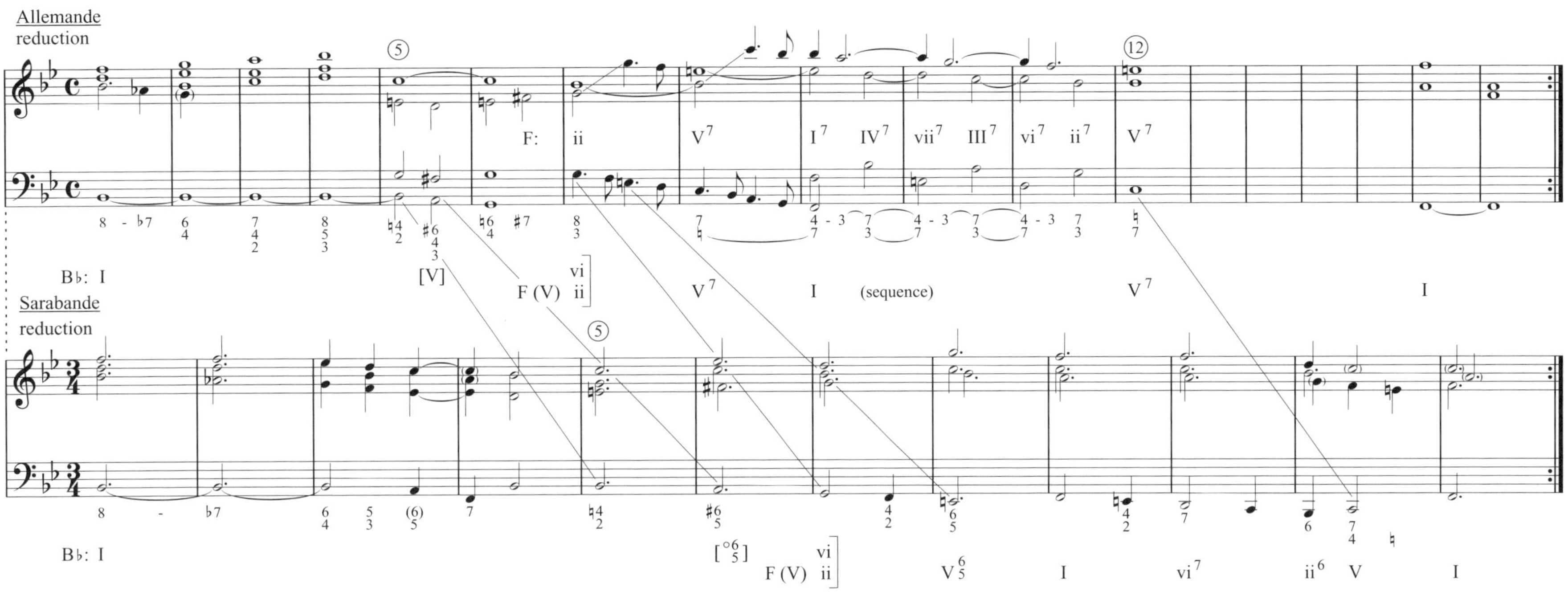

Figure 2.4. Partita I (BWV 825). Comparison of Allemande and Sarabande (part 1)

Minuetta, and Gigue—follow the harmonic scheme outlined in figure 2.7. The main feature of this scheme is the confirmed modulation in part 2 to the submediant (vi) followed by a motion to the subdominant, completing the large-scale descending arpeggiation by thirds as preparation for closure. This is a common tonal paradigm that gains in significance by virtue of its employment as the foundation of all the movements but the Praeambulum and Passepied.[4] Furthermore, there are other features that reinforce the association between the first two movements in this group of five, the Allemande and the Corrente. Most striking are the deceptive delay of closure in the final parts of part 1 of both movements and the ensuing octave descent from d^2 to d^1, as shown at a and b in figure 2.8. Note that the octave progression, also employing the lowered seventh degree of the scale, was heard at the very end of the Praeambulum, as shown at c. Finally, in this regard, note that the final bars of the Corrente, a reduction of which is provided in figure 2.9, provide a diminution of the large-scale harmonic scheme outlined in Figure 2.7 as well as a further example of a descending line—here a tenth—involving the lowered seventh (f♮).

Another clear example of unity created by means of a common harmonic plan occurs in the third cello suite (BWV 1009). As is the case with the fifth partita, several of the movements—in this case the Allemande, Courante, Bourrée I, and Gigue—are related by virtue of a plan involving a confirmed modulation to the submediant in the second part of the binary form.[5] A graphic representation—utilizing both music notation and roman numerals—of how this plan unfolds in each of the four movements is provided in figure 2.10. This figure is organized from simplest (Bourrée I) on the lowest stave to the most elaborate (Gigue) at the top. One can easily see the variants in the manner in which the motion to the

Figure 2.5. Partita I (BWV 825). Large-scale harmonic plans of the Allemande and Sarabande

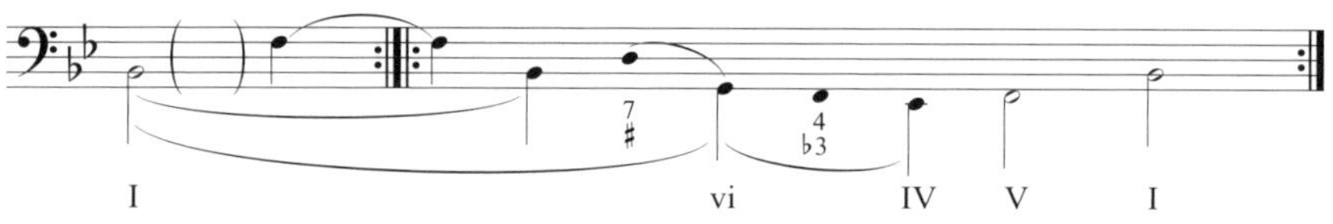

Figure 2.6. Partita I (BWV 825). Large-scale harmonic plan of Menuet II

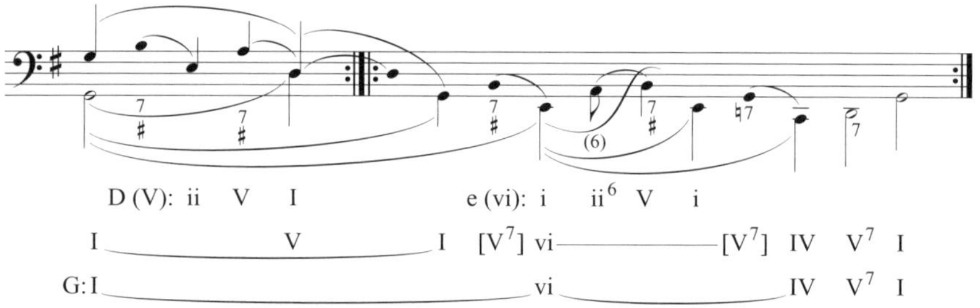

Figure 2.7. Partita V (BWV 829). Common large-scale harmonic plan

Figure 2.8. Partita V (BWV 829)

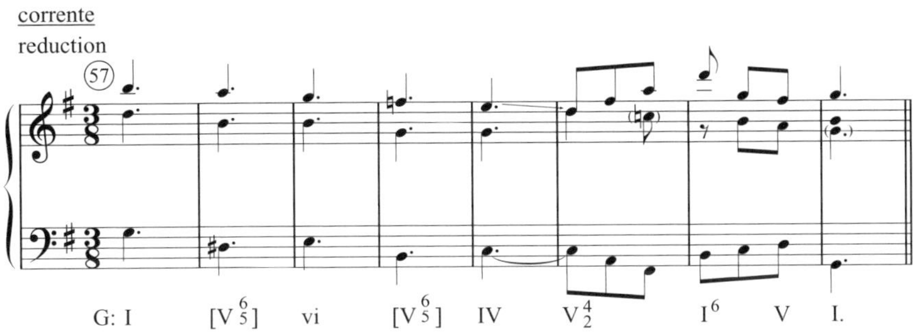

Figure 2.9. Partita V (BWV 829), Corrente, mm. 57–64

dominant at the end of part 1 is achieved. Of greater significance to this discussion are the contents of the second part of the binary form, including the modulation to vi. With the exception of the Gigue, the modulations to the submediant are achieved in much the same way.

Following confirmation of the modulation at the cadence, the simplest of the movements, Bourrée I, progresses directly to II^7 (= V^7 of V) and on to closure. In both the Allemande and the Courante, the progression of harmonies continues in very similar fashion to the subdominant and then to the supertonic, each introduced by their dominants (in one case by a substitute for the dominant, the diminished-seventh chord). Once the modulation to vi is finally confirmed in the Gigue the harmonies progress sequentially through the dominant to the subdominant on its path to closure.

The outline of the harmonic plan of the Gigue (figure 2.10, top system) indicates that the modulation to vi is delayed by a parenthetical digression. The context for that digression is provided in figure 2.11, a reduction of bars 49–72 of the movement. As shown below the reduction, the modulation to vi is prepared in bars 53–56 but not realized until bar 72. In the intervening bars the music first recalls the main key, then its subdominant (F), the eventual goal of the descending arpeggiation by thirds, before reestablishing and confirming the submediant as the immediate goal of modulation. Digressions of this sort add great color while creating tension, and, from an analytic perspective, are far more interesting than passages that are more predictable.

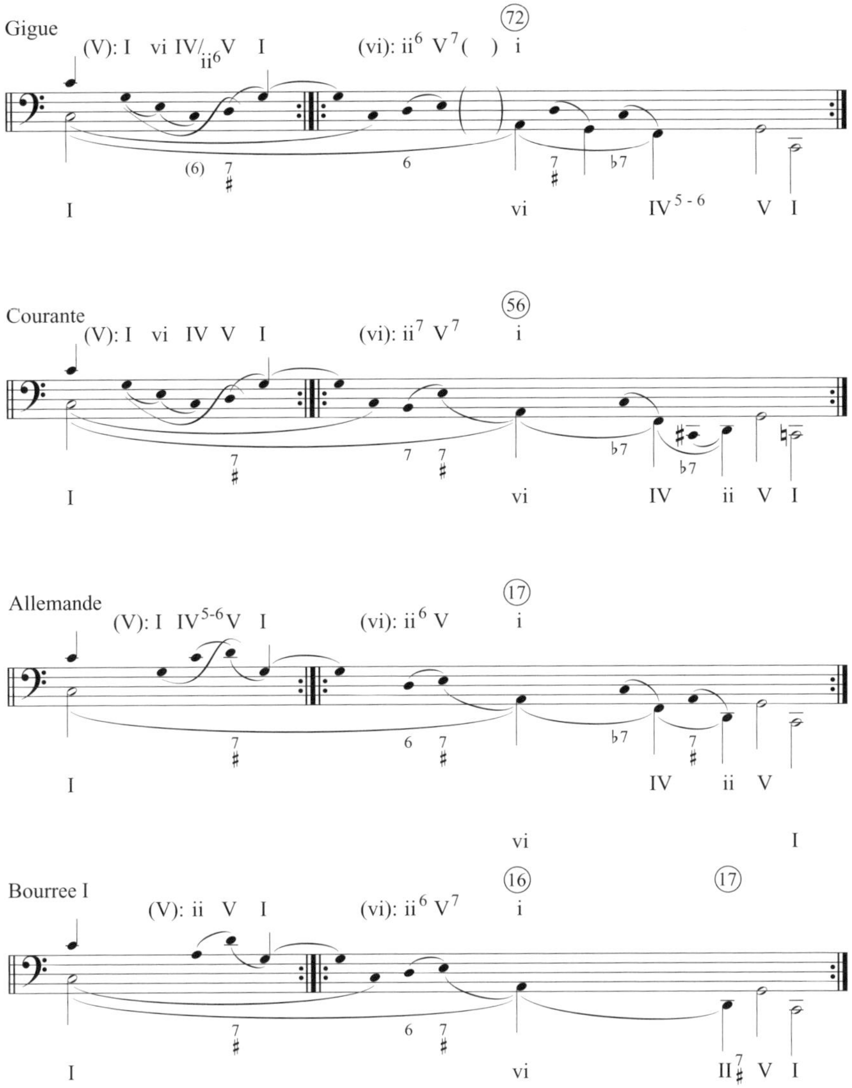

Figure 2.10. Cello Suite III (BWV 1009)

Figure 2.11. Cello Suite III (BWV 1009), Gigue, mm. 49–72

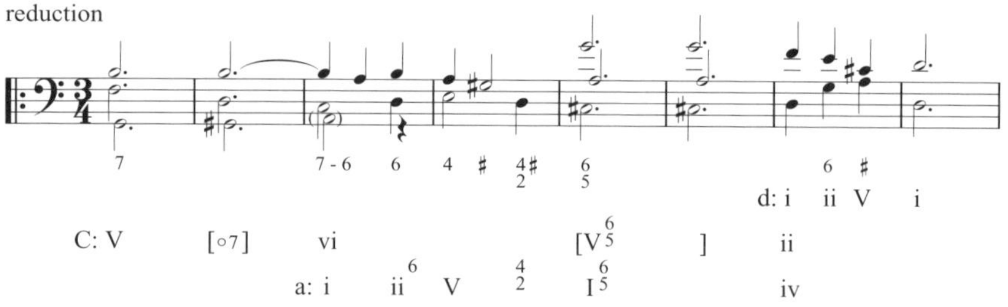

Figure 2.12. Cello Suite III (BWV 1009), Sarabande, mm. 17–24

One technique employed by Bach to avoid a sense of completion is to substitute for the expected chord of resolution or arrival a more active one, like a secondary dominant, thus propelling the music forward. A clear example of this procedure occurs in the second part of the Sarabande of BWV 1009, where Bach once again has carefully prepared a motion to the submediant. We expect completion of this promise, and if our expectation had been fulfilled this would have been yet another movement in this suite, the fifth, to take this path. Instead Bach substitutes for the expected A-minor harmony a six-five chord above c♯, thus propelling the music on to a new goal, which is achieved in bar 24. A reduction of these bars with accompanying harmonic analysis is provided in figure 2.12. Note that the point of substitution (bar 21) coincides with a sudden shift of register, accentuating the necessity for continuation.[6]

So far we have considered only examples in the major mode.[7] For our final example in this group let us turn our attention to a work in E minor, English Suite V (BWV 810). Three movements of this suite—the Allemande, Courante, and Sarabande—share a large-scale harmonic design involving a confirmed modulation to the subdominant (A minor) in part two of the binary form. In addition, these movements share similar melodic characteristics at the background level, and for this reason interpretations of their essential voice-leading structures—Schenkerian graphs of the middleground and background levels—are provided in figure 2.13. Harmonically all three movements progress as expected to the dominant at the cadence closing part 1, through they differ considerably in their details. However, as shown in figure 2.13, this temporary stabilization of the dominant exists within a tonic prolongation, and it is the transformation of this tonic into a major harmony with added seventh in part 2 that leads to the subdominant and from there eventually to the dominant and the close in E minor. From a melodic perspective, all three movements are controlled by a fundamental-line descent from scale degree 3, which is prolonged at the deepest level by its upper neighbor note, first supported by the subdominant and later transformed into a dissonant seventh requiring its return to scale degree 3 and from there its descent to closure. Also note that in all three movements establishment of the first note of the fundamental line occurs several measures into the movement, introduced by what Schenker would label *Anstieg*, a stepwise harmonized ascent of the main melodic line to the initiating tone of the fundamental line. While these three movements share this characteristic, it must be stressed that the composition of the *Anstieg* varies considerably from movement to movement. That is, the three share the same deep-level structure, but differ considerably in their details.

The *Anstieg* in the Allemande is particularly complicated. Scale degree 3 is articulated on the downbeat of bar 2, but with the statement of the right-hand material of bar 1 now in the left-hand part, the melodic line continues its upward projectory to b^2 and from there descends by step to e^2 supported by tonic harmony in bar 4, forming a closed unit prolonging

Figure 2.13. English Suite V (BWV 810). Comparison of Allemande, Courante, and Sarabande

the tonic and e^2, and it is from this point that the structure unfolds. The music moves almost immediately toward the dominant, and by the time the g^2 over e is reached in bar 7, it is no longer heard in relation to the tonic key, but rather in relation to its dominant. That is, by the time g^2 is established as the first note of the fundamental line, the harmony has already moved away from the home key. From this point, the line descends to the inner voice tone b^1 at the cadence. In part two the tonic harmony with g^2 on top is restated prior to its alteration introducing a^2, the upper neighbor note, supported by the subdominant harmony. The cadence in the key of the subdominant occurs in the lower register in bar 17, but the continuation is in the upper register. From a^2 the line descends to $f\sharp^2$ over a prolongation of the subdominant harmony (where the subdominant is transformed into a supertonic harmony by means of the 5–6 motion), but then the a^2 is restated over the dominant harmony before returning to g^2 and on to closure.

From a structural perspective, the Courante is by far the least complex. In this movement g^2 is established as the *Kopfton*, the first note of the fundamental line, in bar 4 in direct relation to the tonic harmony. Harmonically the path to the dominant is divided by a motion to III (G). Melodically the first part is characterized by two descending sixth progressions, the first from the inner-voice tone e^2 (bar 4) to g^1 at the G-major internal cadence and the second from g^2 (implied) in bar 9 to b^1 at the cadence on the dominant. As occurred in the Allemande, g^2, supported by tonic harmony, is restated in part 2 before its chromatic alteration leading to the subdominant supporting the upper neighbor tone a. Here again the cadence is in the lower register, but the continuation is in the upper register. (All cadences prior to the final one—in bars 9, 12, and 16—are in this lower register. This is true in the Allemande as well). The neighbor note is restated in the upper register in bar 21, harmonized by a D-major harmony (VII), before its statement as seventh of the dominant and resolution to g^2 over tonic harmony and immediate continuation to the final cadence.

The Sarabande opens with a two-bar closed unit in the tonic, E minor, which is then stated in modified form a third higher, leading to a brief cadence on III. What follows is a sequence leading to g^2 supported by an E-minor harmony in the second half of bar 6, which becomes the point of departure for the progression to the dominant at the cadence in bar 8. That is, by the time the first note of the fundamental line is established the harmony has already moved away from the home key, similar to what we observed in the Allemande. The E-minor harmony and g^2 are restated in bar 10, from which point the line first progresses down a third to e^2 and then an additional fifth to a^1 at the cadence on iv in bar 16. Recall that the cadences on the subdominant in both the Allemande and Courante occurred in this lower register, followed almost immediately by a return to the upper register. Here, however, the upper register is not regained until bar 21, coinciding with the prolongation of the subdominant (transformed into a supertonic by a 5–6 motion, as occurred in the Allemande) incorporating an ascending sequence connecting a^1 to e^2. Considering what had occurred at the equivalent point in the previous two movements, we might expect closure in the upper register. Instead the neighboring a is transferred to the lower register, as shown in figure 2.13, now as the dissonant seventh of the dominant, leading to closure in the lower register. Note that the final descent is covered by a varied repetition of the opening motivic gesture.

The preceding discussion of three movements from English Suite V (BWV 810) anticipates a topic that will be developed in chapter 4 and is central to the detailed examination of two works in Part II of this study. This example was introduced in this context to illustrate the association of movements from a minor-mode suite by virtue of a common large-scale harmonic scheme, but the similarity goes far beyond the harmonic realm. The three movements share a deep-level structural pattern.

Notes

1. The correspondence between these two movements continues, at least at the macro level, into part 2. Both movements modulate to the subdominant, though in the Courante Bach avoids a cadence on the subdominant at the last minute.

2. Pivot chords between keys are indicated by a single bracket. Roman numerals or other symbols enclosed in square brackets are functions of the subsequent harmony. That is, the symbols [V] vi mean V of vi followed by vi, likewise [$^{\circ}\,{}^{6}_{5}$] vi indicate diminished seventh chord in six-five position of vi followed

by vi. It is possible to extend this method of short-hand notation to include secondary functions other than dominant, for example [ii V] V.

3. Figure 2.5 does not attempt to represent the entire succession of chords but rather the essential harmonies of the two movements. Details of the first part are shown in Figure 2.4.

4. However, the modulation to the submediant (vi) is foreshadowed in the Praeambulum and prepared, though not confirmed, in the Passepied. The completed modulation to the submediant in the Sarabande is particularly interesting in that it involves a parenthetical reference to the tonic, an internal expansion of the phrase, on the way to reaching its goal.

5. The emphasis on the submediant occurs already in the Prelude (bars 24–28), though here the modulation occurs within a tonic prolongation.

6. For an analysis of the complete movement see Heinrich Schenker, "The Sarabande of Bach's Suite No. 3 for solo violoncello [BWV 1009]," trans. Hedi Siegel, in *The Masterwork in Music, A Yearbook*, vol. 2 (1926), ed. William Drabkin (Cambridge: Cambridge University Press, 1996), 55–58.

7. Two additional suites in the major mode that have several movements related by virtue of a common harmonic plan are: 1) French Suite V (BWV 816): Allemande, Courante, Sarabande, Gavotte, Bourrée, and Gigue; and 2) Orchestral Suite I (BWV 1066): Courante, Gavotte I, Bourrée I, Menuet I, and Menuet II. For additional examples in the minor mode, see Partita II (BWV 826), Allemande and Courante, the first parts of which were compared at the beginning of this chapter. In addition, these two movements share not only the same overall harmonic plan but also the same deep-level voice-leading structure. The same relationship exists between the Allemande and Sarabande of Partita VI (BWV 830). Finally, consider English Suite VI (BWV 811): Allemande, Courante, and Gavotte I, the first and last being characterized by their last-minute avoidance of a cadence confirming the modulation to the subdominant in their second parts.

3

Motivic Parallels

THE WORD "MOTIVE" has acquired multiple meanings over the years, and thus it seems prudent to attempt a definition of the term and, by doing so, to clarify its meanings.[1] In its broadest meaning, a motive is a musical idea that is repeated in the course of a composition. Where theorists in the past have differed is in the nature of the idea and, for that matter, in the nature of its repetitions. As a starting point, we might distinguish between two basic types of motive, the rhythmic motive and the pitch motive. Though a rhythmic idea can be subjected to augmentation and/or diminution in the course of a work, repetitions are most often at the same level. Undoubtedly the most famous example of this phenomenon in the classical literature is the rhythmic motive that pervades Beethoven's Fifth Symphony. While this idea is associated with specific pitches at specific points in the composition, it is the rhythm, not the pitch, that defines it as a motivic idea. We have, in fact, already encountered a rhythmic motive in our brief discussion of the Toccata from Partita VI (BWV 830) in chapter 1. The dotted rhythmic figure that opens the partita is repeated within the outer sections of the Toccata itself and reappears in different guises in the Allemanda and Sarabande.

A pitch motive is defined by its specific pitch or scale-degree succession and its contour, but not normally by its rhythmic articulation. To be sure, any given statement will be articulated rhythmically, but that articulation will not necessarily be repeated with successive statements of the motive. What is repeated is the specific succession of pitches, in which case the relationship is called pitch specific,[2] or the specific succession of scale degrees, in which case the relationship is scale-degree specific. Let us consider a simple example, the neighbor-note motive g–a♭–g, scale degrees 5–6–5 in C minor. When this idea is repeated at the same pitch level, it is easily recognized as a parallel statement. But the parallel is also recognized when the motive appears transposed to the dominant: d–e♭–d. What is preserved is the scale-degree succession. There are also cases where the pitch content of two ideas is so similar that it is the contour that differentiates them. We have observed just this situation in our brief encounter with the Menuet from French Suite II (BWV 813). What were identified as motives a and b, originally stated in bars 1 and 5, respectively, are defined by contour. See figure 1.2 and the accompanying discussion in chapter 1.

Repetitions of pitch motives are subject to a greater variety of manipulation than rhythmic ones. Repetitions may be at the same pitch level, or they may be transposed as well as inverted and/or stated in reverse. Perhaps more pertinent to this study, they can appear at different levels of the voice-leading structure. This is an important corollary of Schenker's definition of structural levels. He has shown that a musical idea may appear at different levels, either expanded or contracted in relation to its original appearance.[3] In such cases, recognition of the parallel depends on an understanding of the underlying voice-leading of a musical work. Because these motives, or at least some of their statements, exist at layers below the musical surface, we will refer to them as voice-leading motives to distinguish them from pitch motives that are easily recognizable from their surface articulations. That is, the voice-leading motive is a type of pitch motive whose statements appear at deeper layers of the structure. Examples below will clarify the distinction between these two types.

It is possible that a single pitch class, particularly when it is an alteration of a diatonic scale step and thus has a strong aural impact, may function like a motive. Most common in Bach's style are scale degrees borrowed from the parallel minor: ♭7, ♭6, and ♭3, as well as ♭2. Consider, for example, the use of the so-called Neapolitan sixth chord in the second lute suite (BWV 996). Its reappearance in bars 16–18 of the Gigue clearly recalls its original statements in bars 11 and 64 of the Praeludio. Perhaps a more striking example of the use of ♭2 occurs in Partita III (BWV 827) in A Minor (see figure 3.1). B♭ (♭2), which is first introduced two bars from the end of the opening Fantasia as a melodic embellishment of scale degree 1, becomes a characteristic feature of the Gigue subject. In the intervening movements, B♭ makes several appearances, most frequently as scale degree 6 in the key of the subdominant.[4]

We mentioned briefly in chapter one the employment of ♭6 as a link between the Allemande and Courante movements of the *Praeludium et*

Figure 3.1. Partita III (BWV 827). Uses of ♭2

Partita del tuono terzo (BWV 833). The neighbor-note pattern 5–♭6–5 (g–a♭–g) in the key of the dominant, first introduced in the approach to the cadence at the end of the first part of the Allemande, is repeated at the equivalent spot in the Courante, creating a clear aural connection between the two movements. Also noted previously was the pervasive use of ♭7 in Partita I (BWV 825) most frequently as I♭7 (V^7 of IV). See table 2.1 and the accompanying discussion in chapter 2.[5] A more complex situation involving the juxtaposition of the lowered seventh degree of the scale with the leading tone occurs in several movements from English Suite I (BWV 806). Figure 3.2 provides the music with analytic additions for the following excerpts from that work: Prélude, 1–7; Gigue, 1–7; Sarabande, 1–4; and Allemande, 1–5. The idea that unites the first two of these is the pitch succession a^2–g♮^{2}–f♯^{2}–a^2–g♯^{2}, indicated on the score, in both cases harmonized by the progression $I^{8–♭7}$ IV [V] V. Careful examination of these two passages reveals an even closer relationship than this encompassing voice-leading motive. As shown in the sketches provided in figure 3.3, these two passages also share the following characteristics: 1) imitation at the octave; and 2) the same general voice-leading framework. Note also the secondary emphasis on the inner-voice tone c♯^{2}. As we turn next to the Sarabande, note that it opens with this pitch (c♯^{2}), which we might interpret as an inner-voice tone beneath an implied a^2. If we can

Figure 3.2. English Suite I (BWV 806)

Figure 3.2. (continued)

Table 3.1. Harmonization of the stepwise descent from a^2 to $g\sharp^1$ in bars 1–5 of the Allemande of English Suite I (BWV 806)

a^2–$g\natural^2$–$f\sharp^2$–e^2–d^2–$c\sharp^2$–b^1 - - - - - a^1 - - - - - $g\sharp^1$	
I - - - - (pedal) - - - $[V^4_2]$ V6 [ii V^4_3]	V

accept this a^2 in retrospect as implied by context—a notion that has great significance for our interpretation of the deep structures of three movements from the keyboard suite, BWV 818/818a (chapter 5)—then we can understand the opening of this movement as a condensed statement of the motive identified as the overall voice-leading pattern common to the opening bars of the Prélude and Gigue. Finally, a variant of this idea occurs in the opening bars of the Allemande, where the lowered seventh degree of the scale (g♮)[6] is part of an extended stepwise descent in the top voice-leading from a^2 to $g\sharp^1$. (Note also the interchange between $g\natural^1$and $g\sharp^1$ in the inner voice in bar 3.) As shown in table 3.1, the stepwise connection between the outer-voice tone a^2 and the inner-voice tone $c\sharp^2$ occurs over a tonic pedal (A).

A common type of pitch motive is one based on arpeggiation of the tonic triad. Consider, for example, the statements of the C-minor triad from the second partita (BWV 826) reproduced in figure 3.4. When we

Figure 3.3. English Suite I (BWV 806)

hear the opening chord, there is no reason to attach to it any particular significance, but later, when it is stated in a linear fashion—first in bar 8 of the Sinfonia, then in bar 7 of the Allemande, and finally in the opening bar of the Sarabande—it begins to function more and more like a motivic link. A more obvious example of the arpeggiated triad as motive

Figure 3.4. Partita II (BWV 826)

Figure 3.5. Keyboard Suite (BWV 821)

is found in the early keyboard suite in B♭ (BWV 821). Statements of this basic idea as articulated in the opening bars of the Praeludium, Sarabande, Echo, and Allemande are provided in figure 3.5. The arpeggiation, highlighted by analytical overlay, is clear in the first three, but in the Allemande the arpeggiation is incomplete, consisting only of the third d^2–f^2. A similar situation occurs in the opening statements of the Ouverture and Entrée of the Keyboard suite in F (BWV 820), another early work, as shown in figure 3.6.[7] And, as shown by the sketches in figure 3.7, these motivic links are part of a structural arpeggiation to a^2, the first note of the fundamental line, in both movements. A final example in this category is taken from the first orchestral suite (BWV 1066). As shown in figure 3.8, several of the movements of this work—Ouverture, Courante, Gavotte I, Menuet I, and Passepied I—open with ideas that are all based on arpeggiation of the tonic triad. The Courante and Passapied I are additionally linked by a descending stepwise line connecting the third and root of the chord.

The following three sets of examples illustrate what is defined above as a voice-leading motive, that is, a pitch motive articulated at successive layers of the voice-leading fabric of a composition. In all three cases, the motive is the common neighbor-note paradigm. The first set is taken from the early keyboard suite in G Minor, BWV 822. As shown in figure 3.9, the prolongation of scale degree 5 by its upper neighbor note, harmonized by the progression i $[V^7]$ III, is first stated in the opening bars of the Ouverture.[8] In three succeeding movements what is preserved or at least alluded to is the neighbor-note progression d^2–$e\flat^2$–d^2. This is most clearly stated in the opening bars of the Gavotte en Rondeau and

Figure 3.6. Keyboard Suite (BWV 820)

Figure 3.7. Keyboard Suite (BWV 820)

Figure 3.8. Orchestral Suite I (BWV 1066)

Bourée, though in the former the return to d^2 is delayed until the return of the tonic harmony in bar 5. The situation in the opening bars of the Aria is somewhat different. Here the reference to $e\flat^2$ as upper neighbor note of d^2 is clear enough, but instead of returning directly to scale degree 5, the motion continues on to c^2 as the middle member of a descending third progression.

Another work having several movements united by a neighbor-note motive, in this instance involving scale degrees 3–4–3, is the first cello suite (BWV 1007).[9] The opening bars of six movements—the Prélude, Sarabande, Menuet I, Allemande, Courante, and Gigue—are reproduced

Figure 3.9. Keyboard Suite (BWV 822)

in figure 3.10, and in all but the last of these, the excerpt is followed by a reduction of the voice-leading. The paradigm stated at the opening of the Prélude is replicated in different metric settings in the Sarabande and Menuet I. The voice-leading is more complex in the Allemande, though the main difference, as shown in the reduction, is the addition of the harmony in the second bar, thereby introducing the neighbor note c from above. This change elaborates but does not fundamentally alter the underlying pattern, as is the case in the opening phrase of the Courante, where the pattern receives further elaboration. Finally, the 3–4–3 neighbor-note pattern is clearly stated in bars 3–4 of the Gigue, as indicated by the analytic addition to the music. This is no doubt the clearest example you will find in Bach's suites of linking several movements by means of a simple voice-leading motive.

The neighbor-note motive is also represented in several movements from Partita IV (BWV 828), though in less obvious ways than in the two preceding examples. Figure 3.11 provides the opening bars of five of its movements (Ouverture, Allemande, Courante, Aria, and Sarabande) and figure 3.12 the corresponding voice-leading graphs. The clearest statement of the neighbor-note pattern shared by all movements occurs in the opening bars of the Ouverture in counterpoint to the descending motion in parallel tenths, marked by the curved lines in the graph. The statement of the motive in the Allemande is more elaborate and somewhat obscured by introduction of the upper register, which prepares the continuation from scale-degree three in that register beginning in bar 5. Register also plays an important role in the opening phrase of the Courante, where $\hat{3}$is clearly articulated in both registers. The lower register, where the motive 3–4–3 occurs, is shown as primary, but this motion is covered by an elaborated descending third progression in the upper register. The motive is once again clearly articulated in the opening phrase of the Aria, where the 3–4–3 occurs within a larger motion from $\hat{3}$ to $\hat{2}$ supported by the harmonic progression I to V. While this statement of the motive is relatively clear, the one in the opening bars of the Sarabande is almost completely lost in the complex writing. Here the neighbor-note motive occurs by means of a registral shift in conjunction with a descending stepwise progression from d^2 (inner voice) to $f\sharp^1$. What began as a clearly recognizable feature in the voice-leading of the opening gesture of the partita has become obscured in the

Figure 3.10. Cello Suite I (BWV 1007)

Figure 3.11. Partita IV (BWV 828)

Figure 3.11. (continued)

Sarabande, where it is a feature of the voice-leading, but not easily recognizable as a motivic repetition.

We have twice so far noted the role of the lowered seventh degree of the scale as a motivic component, first as an adjunct to our consideration of harmonic repetition between the Allemande and Sarabande of Partita I in chapter 2 (see table 2.1 and accompanying discussion, p. 16), and earlier in this chapter in reference to the first English Suite (see figures 3.2 and 3.3). A third example of this phenomenon occurs in the fourth cello suite (BWV 1010). We first encounter ♭7 in the Prélude, where it is part of a linear progression that can be represented abstractly as 8–♭7–6–♮7–8. As shown in figure 3.13, this "motive" occurs at least three times within the Prélude itself: first in the opening nine bars, where ♮7–8 is transferred into an inner part; second in bars 11–27, where it is reharmonized; and finally at the end of the movement (bars 82–100).[10] This idea is not repeated *per se* in subsequent movements, but rather the linear motion 8–♭7–6 is extended to form a middle-ground progression of a descending octave that is subsequently repeated. This octave progression is heard most clearly at the opening of the Allemande and the closing of the Courante, as shown by the reductions in figure 3.14. Though the motive 8–♭7–6–♮7–8 from the Prélude is not heard directly here, note that ♭7–6 in the top part in bar 3 of the

Figure 3.12. Partita IV (BWV 828)

Allemande is answered immediately by ♮7–8 in an inner part, suggesting a stronger relationship between the two ideas than just the employment of ♭7.[11] One might also hear this octave line in the closing bars of the Allemande, as indicated in the reduction at (a) in figure 3.15. However, as shown in the voice-leading sketch at (b), the octave descent actually begins one bar earlier (from f^2) within the prolongation of the dominant. The correspondence to the closing bars of the Courante is striking.

Let us return briefly to the first orchestral suite (BWV 1066) for a final illustration in this chapter of an extended voice-leading motive. Earlier in the chapter we demonstrated that five movements from the work share similar opening pitch motives, each progressing either by step or by arpeggiation to scale degree 5 (see figure 3.8). If we now examine the continuation of these motives, we discover that four of the five movements—the Ouverture, Courante, Gavotte I, and Menuet I—also share an extended linear progression in their opening sections: the octave g^2–g^1. Reductions of the appropriate portions of these four movements, with added interpretative markings, are provided in figure 3.16.[12] The octave is most clearly articulated in Gavotte I and Menuet I, perhaps a bit less so in the Courante due to the implied but not explicit statements of scale degree 7 (f^2). In the Ouverture the octave is divided into two segments, 8–7–6–5 and 5–4–3–2–1, separated by eight bars.

In the final two examples in this chapter, but particularly in this last one, we have employed the term "motive" to refer to a repeated linear progression, what Schenker labelled *Zug*. For some this may seem a stretch, though the use is consistent with the very general definition of motive given earlier—a musical idea that is repeated in the course of a composition. No matter what label we may use, it is clear that the octave progressions cited contribute to the sense of unity and coherence in these two works.

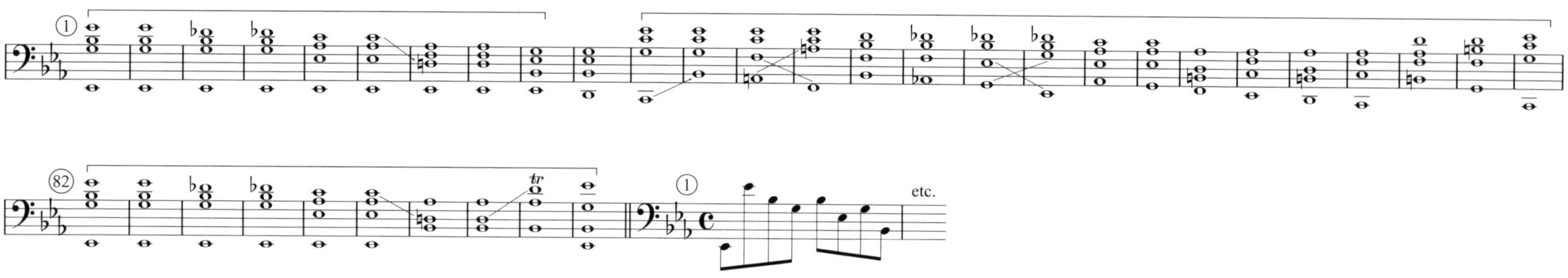

Figure 3.13. Cello Suite IV (BWV 1010), Prélude

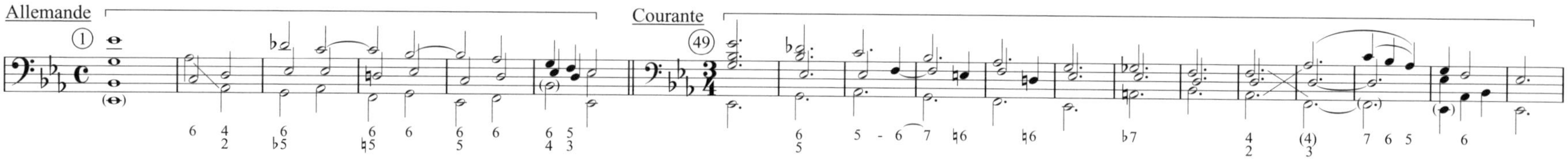

Figure 3.14. Cello Suite IV (BWV 1010). Octave progressions

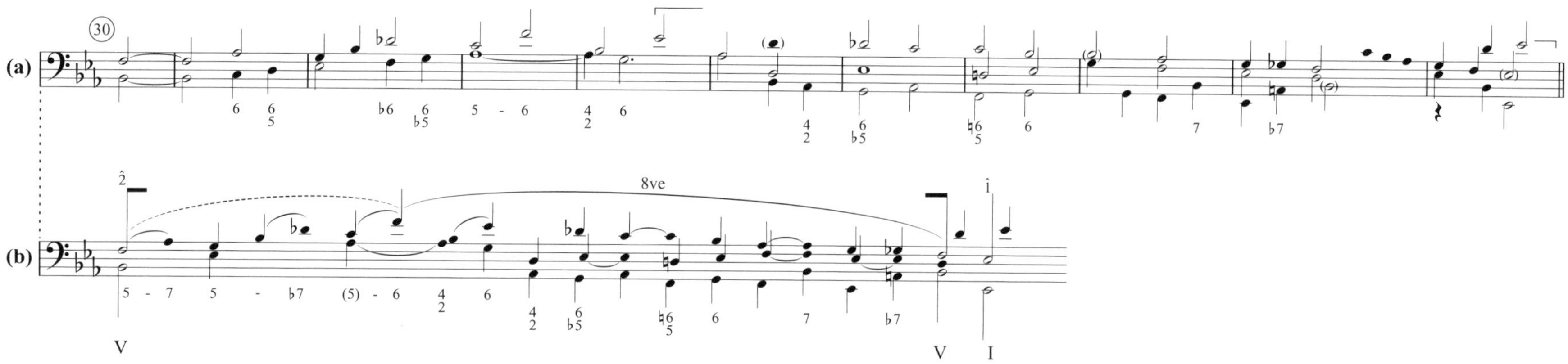

Figure 3.15. Cello Suite IV (BWV 1010), Allemande, mm. 30–40

Figure 3.16. Orchestral Suite I (BWV 1066)

Notes

1. The title of this chapter reflects Schenker's term "motivic parallelism" a concept discussed in depth by Charles Burkhart in his article "Schenker's 'Motivic Parallelisms,'" *Journal of Music Theory* 22, no. 2 (1978): 145–75. It implies a repetition of the motivic idea.

2. Throughout this discussion the term pitch is to be understood as meaning pitch class.

3. For a detailed discussion of Schenker's notion of motive as related to his concept of structural levels, see Burkhart, "Schenker's 'Motivic Parallelisms.'"

4. See the Allemande, 10–11; Corrente, 43; Sarabande, 17–19; Burlesca, 20–23; Scherzo, 15–18 (where we also hear e♭ as ♭2 of D minor); and Gigue, 28, 33, and 47. We also hear b♭ once as scale degree 4 in the key of the submediant (F): Sarabande, 6. Because ♭2 is a feature of the Gigue subject, it is heard again in that context in bars 9 and 21.

5. Another feature that unites particularly the Praeludium and the Allemande of this work is the stepwise motion to the high b-flat (b$\flat^2$) in their opening measures. See also the opening of the Corrente and first Menuet.

6. The lowered seventh degree of the scale also occurs prominently in Courante II and its two Doubles, creating an aural link to the other movements cited.

7. David Schulenberg notes that the "opening gestures of the *overture* and of the *entrée* have similar gestures . . . ," *The Keyboard Music of J. S. Bach* (New York: Schirmer, 1992), 31.

8. The arabic numerals between the staves indicate that the hypermetric structure begins in the second bar following an upbeat bar.

9. This motivic link is noted by David Fuller in the article "Suite" in *The New Grove Dictionary of Music and Musicians*, 2nd ed., 29 vols. (New York: Grove, 2001), 24:665–84.

10. The initial bar of the Prelude has been added at the end of figure 3.13 so the reader can see the pattern (the arpeggiation figure which persists throughout the first part of the movement) from which the reduction is derived. The textures of succeeding movements are more complex and varied. Those readers interested in examining carefully the reductions provided in figures 3.14 and 3.15 will have to consult the score.

11. ♭7 also plays a prominent role in the Sarabande.

12. Compare to figure 2.6, which illustrates the use of the octave progression as a unifying device in Partita V (BWV 829).

4

Structural Associations

THIS CHAPTER IS A CONTINUATION of our investigation into the role of motive as a unifying device in Bach's suites, the focus now being on motive within the context of structural voice-leading. The term "structural" is used here and elsewhere in this work to refer specifically to Heinrich Schenker's concept of structural levels progressing from the *Ursatz* (fundamental structure). It is extremely important that we make a clear distinction between this concept of musical structure and other means of musical organization, like form and key succession. We have already observed the symbiosis of large-scale harmonic organization and voice-leading structure in chapter 2. Several of Bach's suites contain movements that share the same harmonic plan, occasionally at the level of a common figured bass, but more commonly at a much deeper level (e.g., common key succession). In some instances those in the latter group also share the same deep-level voice-leading structure, strengthening the association.[1] We now turn our attention to motive within such a context.

Our first example is taken from the flute partita (BWV 1013). Figure 4.1 provides the opening sections of two of its movements, the Sarabande and the Bourrée anglaise. While each is unique in certain respects, it is also clear that the two openings share several motivic components. Of primary importance in this respect is the fifth a^1–e^2, and secondarily the prolongation of a^1 by its lower neighbor note $g\sharp^1$ and of the e by its upper neighbor note f. In addition, following the prolongation of e^2, both phrases descend by step to b^1 supported by dominant harmony. The Sarabande opens with the ascending fifth a^1–e^2, then returns to a^1 via $g\sharp^1$ before leaping to the metrically and agogically stressed f^1 as the incomplete upper neighbor of the following e^1. From there the line ascends to d^2, which is subsequently decorated by its own third f^2–e^2–d^2 before descending by step to b^1. By contrast, the Bourrée opens with a leap of a descending fifth e^2–a^1, then prolongs a^1 by a progression involving the lower neighbor g♯ before returning to e^2. From there the upper

Figure 4.1. Flute Partita (BWV 1013)

line descends to b^1 while the lower line decorates e^1 by its upper neighbor f^1. So, while each phrase maintains its own character, the two are constructed of the same motivic components[2] and exhibit the same underlying voice-leading.

Figure 4.2 provides voice-leading sketches of the first parts of the Sarabande and Bourrée. Following the initial four-bar phrase of the Sarabande, the initial fifth a^1–e^2 is restated, then each of its elements decorated by their respective neighbor notes, first a^1 by $g\sharp^1$, then e^2 by f^2, which is subsequently reharmonized as the seventh of the dominant leading to the mediant as new support for the return to e^2. This progression occupies another four bars.[3] The melodic line now leaps to g^2, scale degree 5 in the key of the relative major (mediant). From there the overriding voice-leading progression is a descending fifth g^2–c^2, indicated in the sketch by the beam.[4] Covering this progression is a secondary line leading to the high c (c^3).

Figure 4.2. Flute Partita (BWV 1013). Comparison of Sarabande, mm. 1–16, and Bourrée anglaise, mm. 1–20

The sketch of the first part of the Bourrée reveals its close association with the Sarabande. Following the restatement of the tonic harmony in bar 5, the Bourrée progresses directly to g^2 supported by the mediant via a (5)–6 progression. From a metric perspective, this motion extends the initial phrase by two bars, replacing the second four-bar group of the Sarabande. The remainder of the first part (bars 7–20) can be understood as an expansion of the equivalent portion of the Sarabande. That is, what had occupied eight bars in the Sarabande now occupies fourteen bars. The overall progression is once again the descending fifth g^2–c^2, embedded within which is the covering ascent to the high c (c^3). This latter gesture, which now occupies ten bars, is expanded first by repetition of the opening two-bar segment and overlapping—added upper thirds—supported by chromatic passing tones (secondary dominants) in the bass. The details have changed, but the underlying voice-leading remains the same.[5]

The Overture in the French Style (BWV 831) presents a different situation altogether. Here the common thread uniting several of the movements is not a recognizable motive but the underlying voice-leading of their opening statements. As shown in figure 4.3, seven movements of this work are related in this way. At the most basic level the common feature is the delayed establishment of the primary tone d^2 ($\hat{3}$),[6] though movements share other characteristics as well. A brief description of the underlying voice-leading of the opening bars of each of the seven movements follows.

An important feature of the opening of the Ouverture is the descending tetrachord in the bass, above which there is an inner line, beginning with the d^2 in bar 1, progressing in parallel tenths. The top line, beginning with $f\sharp^2$ in bar 2, descends by step to the primary tone d^2 in bar 5.

The clearest relationship to the opening movement occurs in Bourrée II. Once again we have the descending tetrachord in the bass and an inner line progressing parallel to it a tenth above. The upper line, beginning from the opening $f\sharp^1$ progresses by means of a series of 7–6 suspensions in relation to the bass (also derived from the opening movement), and at the last moment the passing tone e is transferred to the upper register to introduce the primary tone d^2 on the downbeat of bar 5.

The voice-leading of the opening of the Courante varies in some respects from the two movements just described, though one basic feature, the descending tetrachord, remains. Here, following the initial

Figure 4.3. Overture in the French Style (BWV 831)

Courante

Bourrée I

Figure 4.3. (continued)

Echo

Figure 4.3. (continued)

Sarabande

Gavotte I

Figure 4.3. (continued)

extension of the tonic harmony (bars 1–3), the descending bass supports a stepwise ascent to the primary tone (d^2), what Schenker would describe by the term *Anstieg*. So, in this case, the primary tone is approached by step from below rather than from above, as occurs in both the Ouverture and Bourrée II.

Bourrée I maintains the *Anstieg* to $\hat{3}$ supported by the bass motion b–a♯–b rather than the descending tetrachord pattern. Note the double neighbor-note decoration of $f\sharp^1$ in the inner voice, which is a feature of the Courante and Gavotte I as well as the Ouverture.

The Echo also introduces the primary tone by an ascending step progression, in this instance progressing to the e^2 to introduce d^2 from above. The harmonization of the elaborated *Anstieg* involves a descending progression by thirds connecting tonic and scale degree 4 in the bass as preparation for the confirming cadence.

The opening gestures of the Sarabande and Gavotte I also share some characteristics with the five others just described. The approach to the primary tone in the Sarabande is by means of a stepwise ascent, though missing the initial b^1. The descending tetrachord appears in the detail of an inner voice, and the bass harmonization of the *Anstieg* is the same b–a♯–b as heard in Bourrée I. The controlling bass of the Gavotte I excerpt is the same as in the opening of the Echo. Here the primary tone is introduced directly after the bass has begun its descending arpeggiation. Note also the elaboration of the inner-voice tone $f\sharp^1$ by its upper and lower neighbors, a characteristic of the Courante and Bourrée I movements as well as the opening gesture of the Ouverture.

Including this discussion of characteristics common to the opening statements of these movements under the general rubric of "motive" may appear a stretch to some readers. Certainly we are not talking about motive in the traditional sense, but rather voice-leading patterns—repeated voice-leading patterns—as motive. Whatever label is most appropriate to assign to the relationships just described, it is clear that these relationships provide audible links among several movements of this work.

Three of the four principal movements from the first violin partita (BWV 1002) open with a similar motivic pattern, the neighbor-note figure $f\sharp^2$–g^2–$f\sharp^2$, and once we look beyond the surface we discover other common features as well. Figure 4.4 provides both the music and corresponding voice-leading sketches of the opening bars of the four movements: Allemanda,

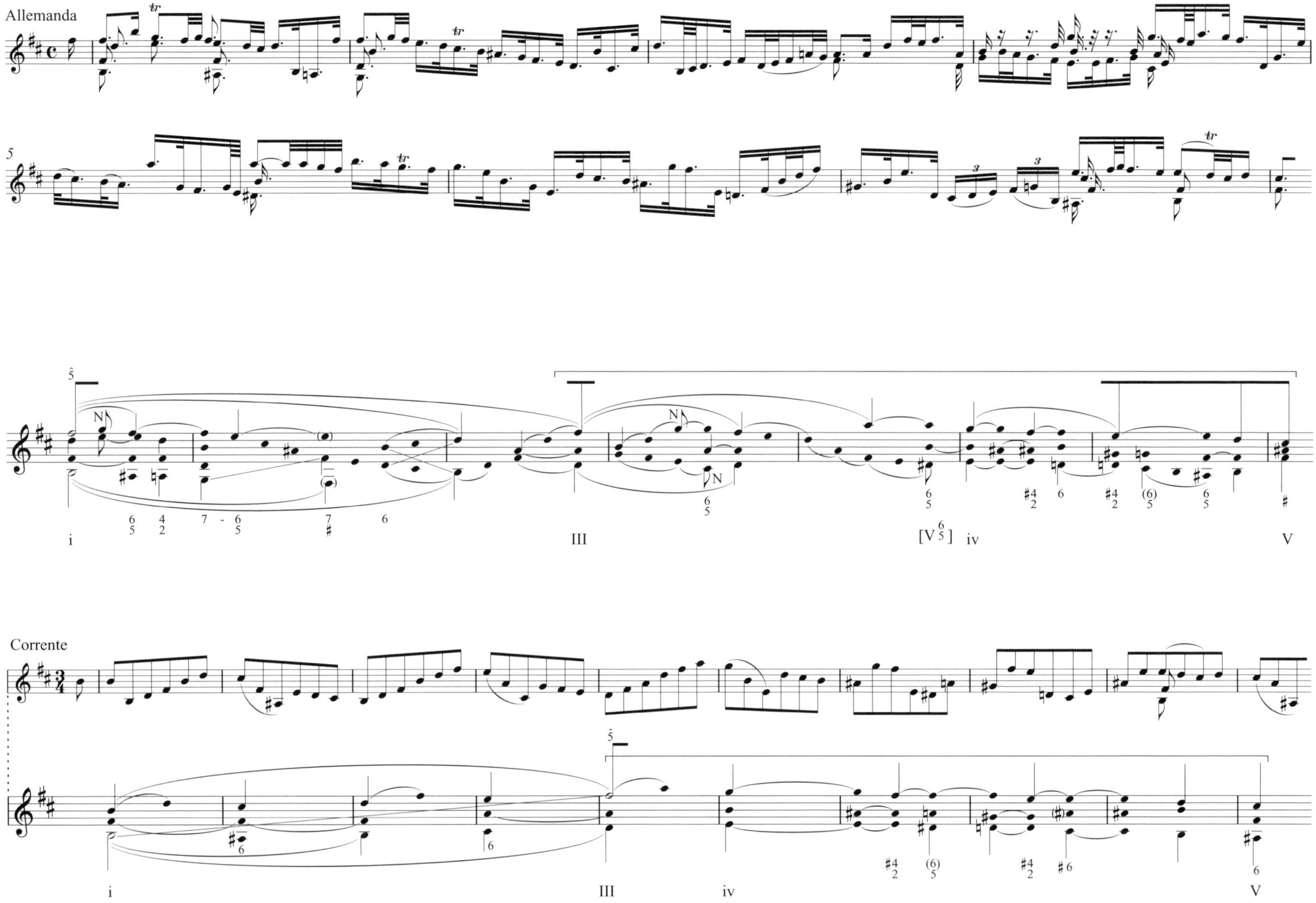

Figure 4.4. Violin Partita I (BWV 1002)

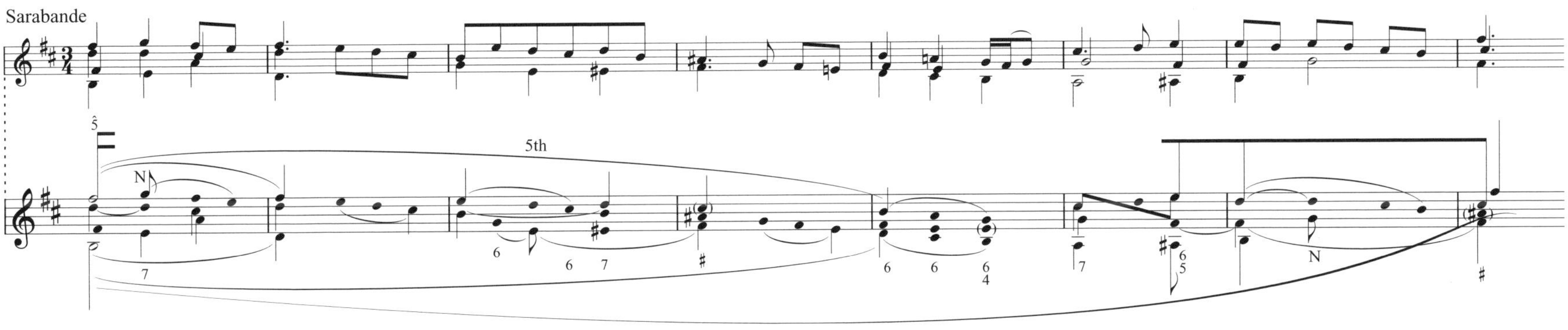

Figure 4.4. (continued)

Corrente, Sarabande, and Tempo di Borea. Following an initial statement of the neighbor-note motive in the top part, the Allemanda descends from the primary tone $f\sharp^2$ ($\hat{5}$) to d^2 within a tonic prolongation before $f\sharp^2$ is reinstated, now supported by the mediant harmony, followed by a second statement of the neighbor-note figure. From this point a^2 is overlapped above $f\sharp^2$ to approach g^2 from above, and from there the line descends to $c\sharp^2$ supported by the dominant. The top line in these bars, $f\sharp^2$–a^2–g^2-$f\sharp^2$–e^2–d^2–$c\sharp^2$, is marked with a bracket since it is repeated in slightly varied form in the next movement. The Corrente opens in a very different fashion, with a stepwise ascent (*Anstieg*) to $\hat{5}$ and once $f\sharp^2$ is attained on the downbeat of bar 5 a varied repetition of the bracketed idea follows. Note the close correspondence between the harmonization in the Allemanda and in the Corrente.[7] The Sarabande opens with a statement of the neighbor note, with $f\sharp^2$ first being harmonized by the tonic and the return by the mediant, recalling in one gesture the two supports given to the primary tone in the initial bars of the Allemanda—at bars 1 and 3–4. The line then descends by step to $c\sharp^2$, first in bar 4 (implied) and again in bar 8. Finally, we have yet another appearance of the $f\sharp^2$–g^2–$f\sharp^2$ figure in the initial phrase of the Tempo di Borea, followed by an elaborated descent of a fifth from the primary tone $f\sharp^2$ to b^1.

The two movements of this work most closely related at deeper levels of structure, though in fact not in the detail of their progressions, are the Allemanda and the Sarabande. Middleground-background sketches of these two movements, aligned to highlight the correspondences, are provided in figure 4.5. Let us begin with the Sarabande, since it is the less complex of the two. Following the opening statement of the neighbor-note motive (not shown in figure 4.5), the line first descends a fifth from the primary tone $f\sharp^2$ to the inner voice tone b^1, a motion that is embedded within the overall progression of a descending fourth from $f\sharp^2$ to $c\sharp^2$ within the first part. After the double bar, the dominant in four-two position returns to the tonic, now in six-three position with b^2 in the

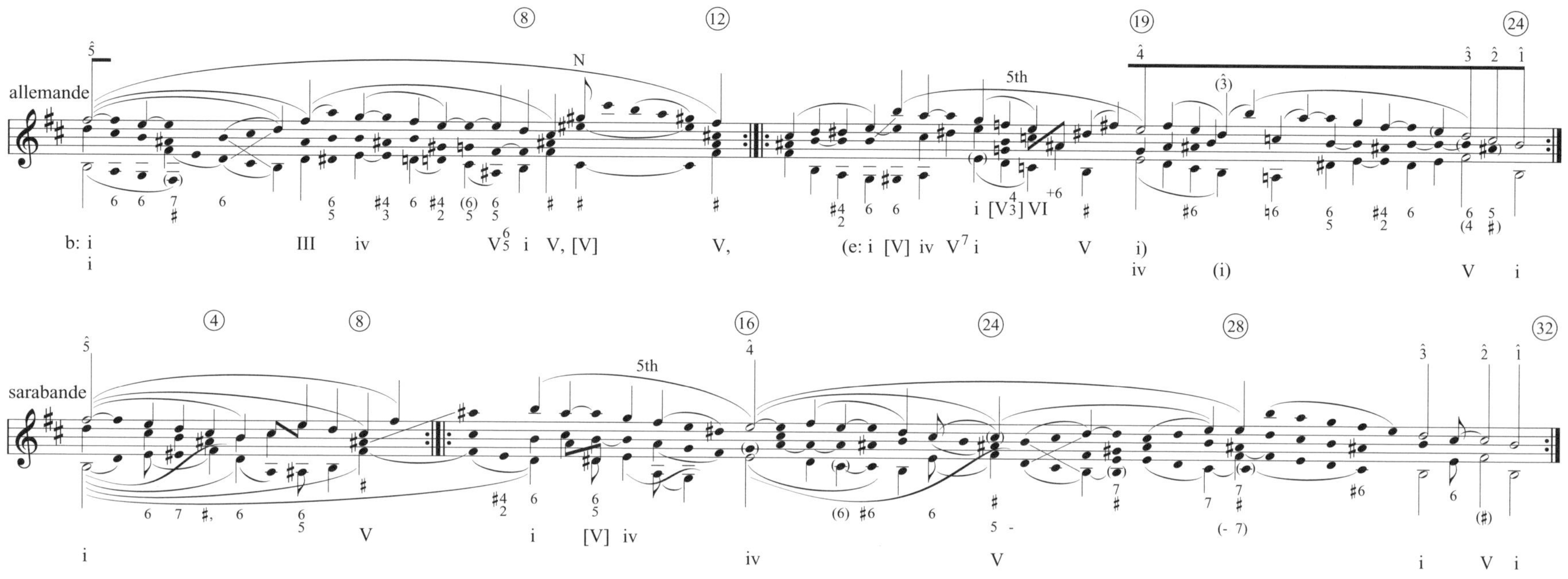

Figure 4.5. Violin Partita I (BWV 1002), Allemanda and Sarabande

top part, and from there the line descends a fifth to scale degree 4 of the fundamental line, harmonized by the subdominant. Over the next six bars the bass descends by step to the tonic, which provides consonant support for the passing tone d^2 within the descending third e^2–d^2–($c\sharp^2$). The goal of this eight-bar phrase is the dominant, which is subsequently prolonged until e^2 is reinstated and finally resolved to d^2 $(\hat{3})$ in bar 30 immediately prior to closure at the cadence in bars 31–32.[8]

The Allemanda, which, as noted above, opens with the neighbor-note figure, initially descends a third from the primary tone $f\sharp^2$ within a prolonged tonic harmony, and then from a reinstated $f\sharp^2$, now harmonized by the mediant, descends via the progression discussed above to the inner tone $c\sharp^2$, supported by the dominant, in bar 8. The following four bars confirm the dominant as the goal of part one and reinstates $f\sharp^2$ as primary via $g\sharp^2$. Thus the opening motive $f\sharp^2$–g^2–$f\sharp^2$ has been expanded and transformed into $f\sharp^2$–$g\sharp^2$–$f\sharp^2$ encompassing the entire first part. In comparing the two movements to this point we see that they correspond only in their larger goals, not in the details of their progressions. Following the double bar, the inner voice tone b^1 is transferred to the upper register and the line descends a fifth from b^2 to scale degree four of the fundamental line, supported by the subdominant harmony. The correspondence to the equivalent passage in the Sarabande is striking despite the differences in the details of the voice-leading. What follows also bears a resemblance to the Sarabande. From the cadence on the subdominant (bar 19), the bass descends by step to the tonic supporting d^2, but here too the motion continues beyond this point until the cadence at the close of the phrase.

The final set of examples in this chapter is drawn from the extraordinary second violin partita (BWV 1004) in D Minor. A basic idea common to several of its movements is the stepwise ascent (*Anstieg*) to the primary tone f^2 $(\hat{3})$. Also of significance is the neighbor-note motive a–b♭–a (inner voice) and the persistent idea $b\flat^2$–a^2–g^2–f^2 resulting from transfer of the inner line to the upper register to reintroduce f^2 from above. This latter idea is highlighted by brackets in figure 4.6,

Giga

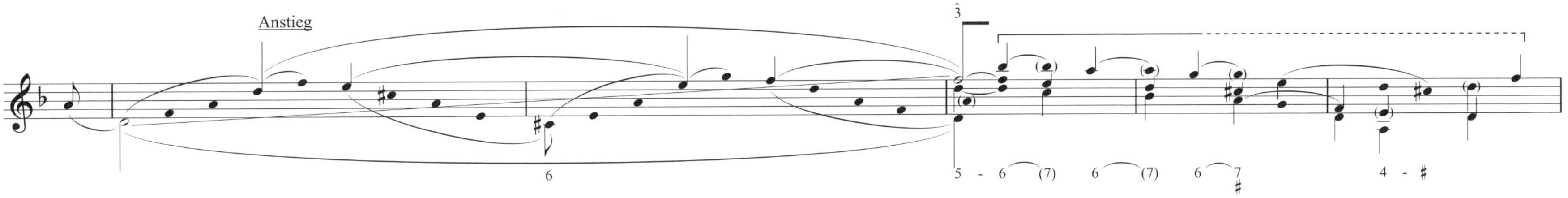

Ciaccona

Figure 4.6. Violin Partita II (BWV 1004)

Allemande

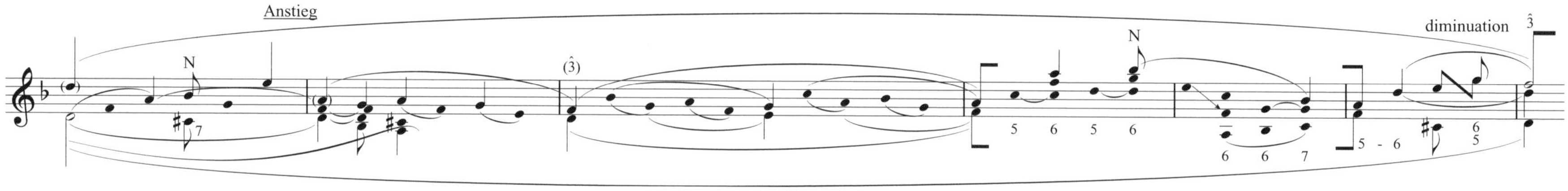

Corrente

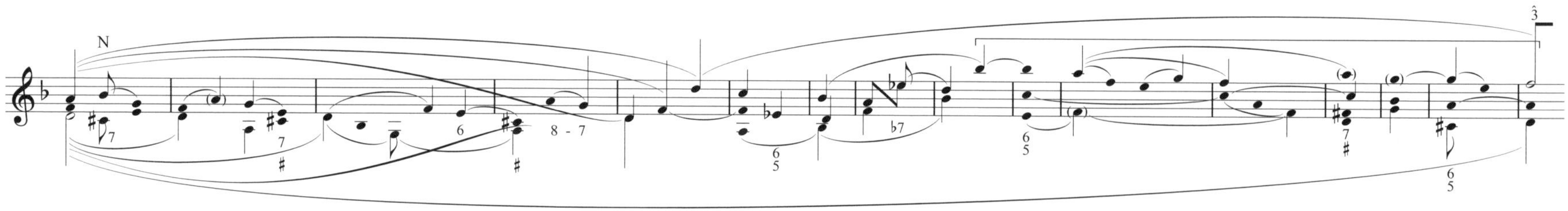

Figure 4.6. (continued)

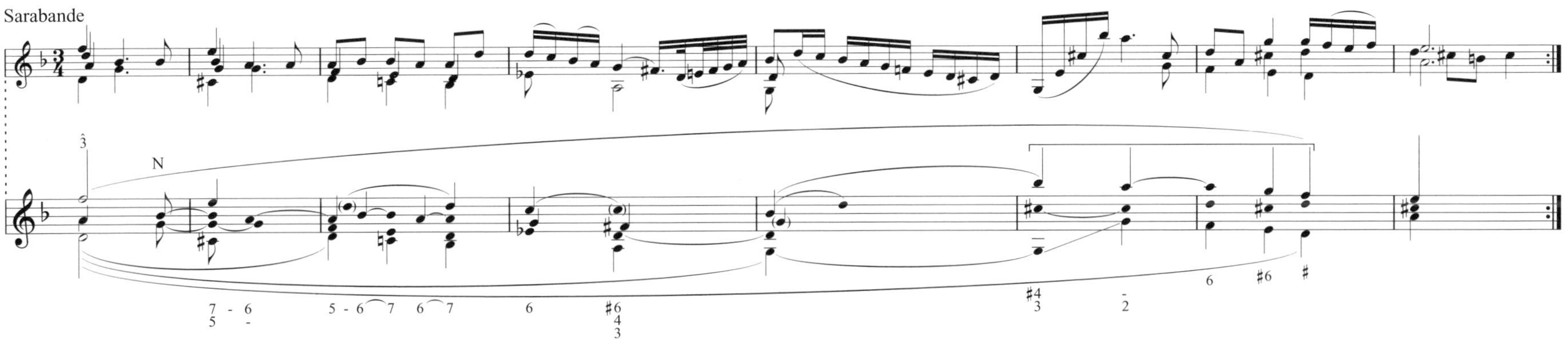

Figure 4.6. (continued)

which provides both music and sketches of the opening bars of all five movements.

The *Anstieg* to $\hat{3}$is most clearly articulated in the Giga. Following the establishment of the primary tone on the downbeat of bar 3, the inner line is transferred to the upper register and f^2 reinstated by means of a descent from $b\flat^2$.

The Chaconne opens with a leap from the inner voice tone a^1 to e^2, reminiscent of the same gesture at the opening of the Allemanda, and when e^2 progresses directly to f^2, the primary tone, it may be understood in retrospect to come from an implied d^2. This rising motion covers a statement of the neighbor-note motive a^1–$b\flat^1$–a^1. The ascent to $\hat{3}$is followed by a statement of the b♭–a–g–f idea in the lower register, but when the opening four bars are repeated in varied form, this idea is transposed to the upper register leading to f^2 on the downbeat of bar 9.

As noted above, the Allemanda opens in a very similar fashion as the Chaconne, except here the harmonies are composed in a linear fashion. The leap to e^2, covering the inner voice statement of the neighbor-note motive, may once again be understood as coming from an implied d^2. Here, however, f^2 does not follow immediately, as in the Chaconne. Though f does follow in the lower register (f^1), the result of a descent from the inner voice tone a^1, the *Anstieg* is not completed until the downbeat of bar 7 following a diminution of that motion.

In the Corrente the primary tone f^2 is not reached until bar 16, and it is not introduced by an ascending linear motion but by large-scale arpeggiation: a^1 (bar 1)–d^2 (bar 5)–f^2 (bar 16). Motivic parallels to the other movements are clear. Note the neighbor-note motive a^1–$b\flat^1$–a^1 at the beginning and the introduction of f^2 by the descending stepwise motion $b\flat^2$–a^2–g^2–f^2. Though not stated here as a continuous line, as it is later in the partita, this is, in fact, the first time we hear this important idea in this work.

The Sarabanda differs from the other movements in that f^2, the primary tone, is stated immediately at the beginning. Despite this difference, motivic references to the other movements are clear. Note once again the neighbor note motive in the inner voice at the beginning and the transfer of b♭ to the upper register in bar 6 followed by a statement of the $b\flat^2$–a^2–g^2–f^2 idea. In this case the descending motion continues beyond f^2 to e^2 supported by the dominant harmony at the cadence.[9]

Structural associations among movements of the D-minor Partita also exist at deeper—that is, at more remote—levels than just described. Figures 4.7, 4.8, and 4.9 provide sketches of the Allemanda, Corrente, and Sarabanda, respectively. Comparison of the first two of these reveals that they are based on the same underlying model, which consists of the following features subsequent to the establishment of the primary tone f^2. First the top voice descends a sixth from f^2 to a^1 at the cadence on the

Figure 4.7. Violin Partita II (BWV 1004), Allemanda

dominant at the end of part 1 of the binary form. The outer-voice tone e², either stated explicitly or implied by context at this point, is stated immediately after the double bar and returned to f² and the tonic harmony, forming a tonic prolongation that incorporates the preceding formal division at the dominant. Next the top voice progresses via the chromatic passing tone f♯² to g² at the internal cadence on the subdominant, and from there the line descends a third to scale degree 2, supported by dominant harmony, and on to closure.

The opening of the Allemanda—the stepwise ascent to the primary tone f²—has already been described. From bar 7 the line descends a sixth to the inner-voice tone a¹ at the cadence. (Not shown in this sketch is the considerable activity in the upper register. In other words, only the most essential features of the voice-leading structure are indicated here.) In this case the outer-voice tone e² is stated explicitly at the cadence, then restated after the double bar in preparation for the return to f² and the tonic harmony. The chromatic motion through f♯² to g² is elaborated by a descending motion from f² into the inner voice, eventually arriving at b♭¹ at the subdominant cadence (bar 23), and by the descending third introducing f♯². Figure 4.7 shows that the following motion to the mediant (F) in bar 27, which provides consonant support for the implied passing tone f², falls within a prolongation of the subdominant ($\text{iv}^{5-\flat 6}$) leading to the dominant supporting scale degree 2 and subsequent closure at the cadence in bars 31–32.

As shown in figure 4.8, the main line of the Corrente descends a sixth to the inner-voice tone a¹ (implied but not stated) at the cadence on the dominant following the establishment of the primary tone f² in bar 16. The parallel to the Allemanda is clear, though of course the details and character differ. The return to f² and the tonic harmony occurs in bar 28,

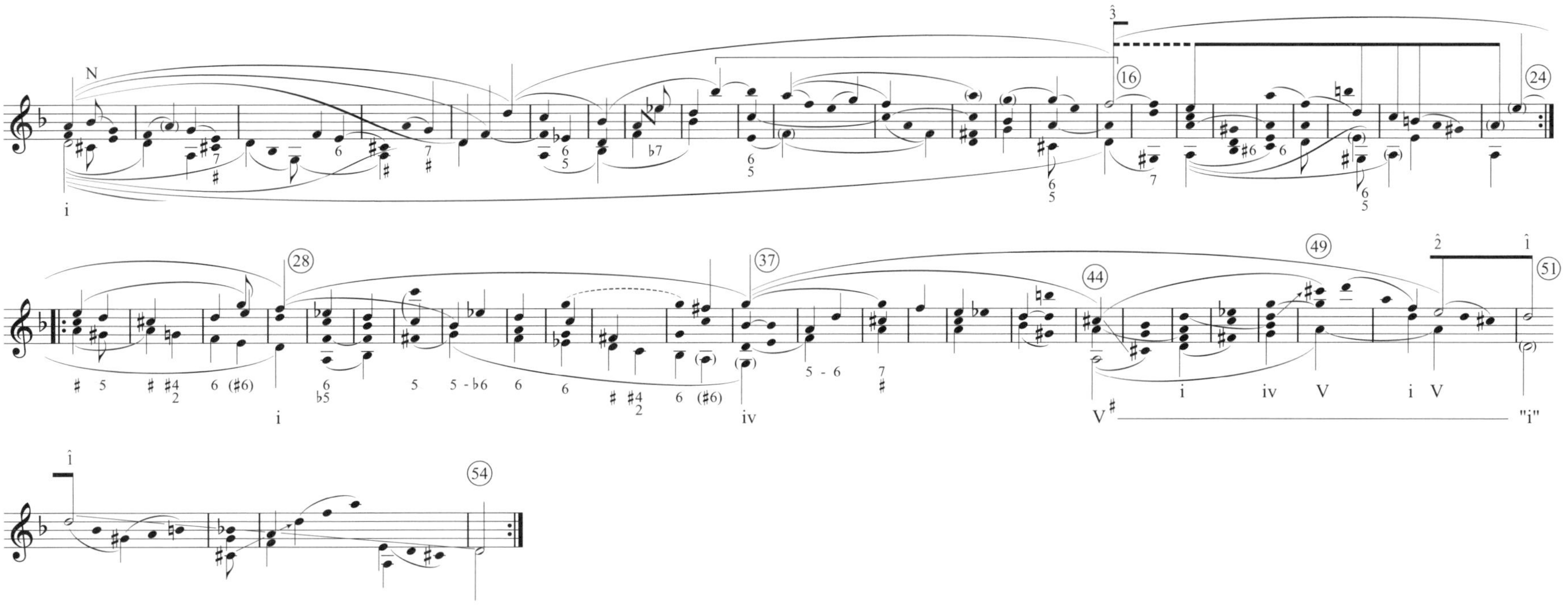

Figure 4.8. Violin Partita II (BWV 1004), Corrente

and from f^2 the line descends to the inner-voice tone $b\flat^1$ at the subdominant cadence as the upper line progresses through the chromatic passing tone $f\sharp^2$ to g^2. Again the parallel is clear. The subsequent prolongation of g^2 and its transformation from a stable pitch, supported by the subdominant harmony, to an unstable pitch, as seventh of the dominant, occurs in bars 37–49. Connection of the seventh to the fifth of the dominant harmony $(\hat{2})$ occurs through the consonant passing tone f^2 in bar 50, supported by tonic harmony, as the melodic line progresses toward closure. However, harmonic closure is avoided at the last minute and the motion is directed beyond that point to the cadence on d^1 in bar 54.

Figure 4.9 provides a sketch of the Sarabanda, revealing structural connections (as well as differences) between this movement and the previous two. Following the repeat, e^2 is not returned to f^2 and tonic harmony, as occurred in the Allemanda and Corrente, but is prolonged through bar 12, where it is supported by a C-major harmony. From there the approach to the cadence on the subdominant (bar 16) is reminiscent of the equivalent passages in the other two movements. The top part, from e^2, splits into two lines, one descending by step to $b\flat^1$ at the cadence and the other progressing to g^2 via $f\sharp^2$. Note the approach to g^2 via a chromatic version of the voice-leading motive $b\flat^2$–a^2–g^2–f^2, highlighted in the sketch by the bracket. The subsequent prolongation of g^2 and the subdominant harmony, transformed by the indicated 5–♭6 motion, is related to the equivalent passage in the Allemanda.[10] Following a final statement of the $b\flat^2$–a^2–g^2–f^2 idea, the line progresses to closure in the upper register.

Let us review briefly what we have discovered so far about intermovement connections in the Bach suites. First, it is important to

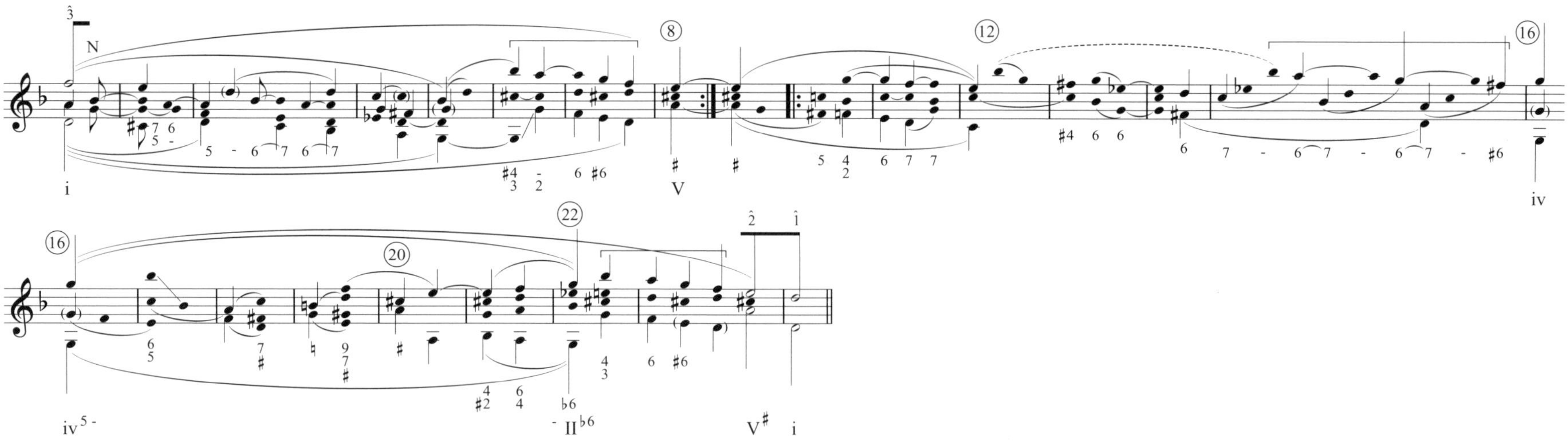

Figure 4.9. Violin Partita II (BWV 1004), Sarabanda

reiterate that some, but not all, the suites exhibit inter-movement associations beyond the obvious feature of a common tonality. Some may be collections of individual movements in the same key, while others clearly must have been written at one time as integrated works. Second, of those works that do exhibit inter-movement connections, no single compositional technique emerges as dominant. Rather there seems to be a multiplicity of approaches, in some instances operating alone and in other cases working in combination. We have seen clear examples of two or more movements of a suite being connected by means of common surface characteristics, e.g., common motives or figured-bass patterns. We have also observed the opposite, that is, suites with movements exhibiting common large-scale plans, harmonic and/or structural, with or without recognizable surface repetitions in common. Clearly the most unified are those, like the D-minor Violin Partita, that are highly integrated at multiple levels. Multiple levels of inter-movement connections are attributes of the two works to be examined in Part II, the Keyboard Suite in A Minor (BWV 818a) and French Suite VI (BWV 817).

Notes

1. See Figure 2.13 and the accompanying discussion in chapter 2 of the Allemande, Courante, and Sarabande from the fifth English Suite (BWV 810). Also see note 7 in that chapter, p. 25.

2. The common motivic components—the fifth a^1–e^2 and the neighbor notes g♯[1] and f^2–are clearly articulated in the opening movement, the Allemande, though in that movement the primary tone is $\hat{3}(c^3)$ not $\hat{5}(e^2)$.

3. Numbers above the staff indicate the metric groups. Those interested in reading more about metric organization in relation to the phrase in tonal music should consult William Rothstein, *Phrase Rhythm in Tonal Music* (New York: Schirmer, 1989).

4. Both the Allemande and the Bourrée are written in rounded binary form, that is, with a clear return to the opening material in conjunction with the return to the tonic harmony. The descending-fifth progression in the relative major that closes part 1, when transposed to the tonic in this last part, becomes the vehicle of the final descent of the fundamental line to closure.

5. While the second parts of these two movements share several feature, the close correspondence is not continued throughout.

6. The purpose of the diagonal line connecting the opening bass note and the later established primary tone (Schenker's *Kopfton*) in all seven sketches is to show that they are conceptually related.

7. This correspondence is noted by Joel Lester in *Bach's Works for Solo Violin* (New York: Oxford University Press), 142–43.

8. My colleague Edward Laufer provided several very helpful suggestions regarding the structural organization of this movement.

9. Joel Lester recognizes the tight connections uniting the movements of this work, but by focusing on thoroughbass he misses the important motivic and structural connections. See *Bach's Works for Solo Violin*, example 6.3 and the accompanying discussion.

10. From an analytic perspective the A-major harmony in bar 20 presents an interesting interpretative choice. One possibility is that it is the structural dominant supporting scale degree two (e^2) of the fundamental line. The other is that it is passing within the extended subdominant/flat supertonic ($iv^{5-\flat 6}$) harmony, as shown in figure 4.9. One might make the case for the first of these on the basis of the prevailing four-bar hypermetric organization, as follows:

```
                 16          20          24
||: 1 2 3 4, 1 2 3 4,  1 2 3 4,  1 2 3 4 :||
                 iv          V♯          i
```

However, Bach avoids articulating bar 20 as a point of sub-arrival by continuing the motion beyond that point. In other words, we do not hear a subdivision of this eight-bar phrase into four-plus-four. The potentially confusing factor here is the apparent stalling of motion in bar 21 if the performer plays the rhythm as written. If, on the other hand, the performer arpeggiates the chords in bar 21 as written out in the first half of the next bar, then the motion is directed through to the ♭II harmony.

Part II

5

Keyboard Suite in A Minor (BWV 818a)

THE KEYBOARD SUITE in A Minor is a relatively early work. According to David Schulenberg, it "seems to occupy a stylistic position between the English Suites and the First French Suite,"[1] though it may well have been written much earlier. It exists in two versions, BWV 818 and 818a, both transmitted to us through copies. The earlier version is preserved in two copies, one in the hand of his student, Heinrich Nicolas Gerber, the other anonymous, both dating from the early 1720s. This version consists of five movements: Allemande, Courante, Sarabande simple, its Double, and Gigue. The later version (818a) adds a Prelude, marked "Fort gai," and in place of the original Sarabande–Double pair provides a variant of the Sarabande simple and a Menuet. This version is based on two surviving copies dated much later, around 1740. The following discussion focuses on this later version.

The movements of BWV 818a are related in a variety of ways and at multiple levels. With the exception of the Prelude and the Allemande, each movement opens with a variant of a common underlying pitch motive, the arpeggiation of the tonic triad (a^1–c^2–e^2), most frequently with decoration of the tonic by its lower neighbor note, g♯^{1}, and the fifth by its upper neighbor, f^2. The initial bars of all movements but the Allemande are reproduced in figure 5.1. Each of these ideas, though based on a common underlying pitch motive, is unique, expressing its own character. Still the connecting thread is there, and this thread becomes more pronounced when we examine the voice-leading of the opening phrases of these movements. As shown in figure 5.2, four of them—the Prelude, Sarabande, Menuet, and Gigue—open with harmonized descents of a sixth from e^2 to g♯^{1}. The Courante differs only in that its opening phrase is harmonically closed, supporting a descent of a fifth from e^2 to a^1. Note the employment of f^2 at various levels as a local neighbor note, complete or incomplete, harmonized or unharmonized, and in one instance (the Menuet) extended over several bars.

Similarities among the movements of BWV 818a extend to the harmonic sphere, an aspect of unity to be addressed here in relation to structure, since harmonic associations frequently coincide with similarities in background-level voice-leading. It is important as we approach the matter of background structure in this work to make a clear distinction between motivic design and voice-leading structure. The two may coincide, but in this instance they do not. As we have seen, the common motivic link among several of the movements is the fifth e^2–a^1, and one might expect the fundamental line to follow this path. But, in fact, it appears as if several of the movements exhibit near-identical fundamental structures involving the descent of an octave, not the fifth. There are at least two important issues associated with this interpretation that require comment, the first having to do with the structure of the fundamental descent from scale degree 8 in the minor mode. It is the descending form of the scale.[2] The second involves consideration of potential variance of this structure. Perhaps the best way to approach

Figure 5.1. Keyboard Suite in A Minor (BWV 818a), Opening bars of the Prelude, Courante, Sarabande, Menuet, and Gigue

Figure 5.1. (continued)

this matter is to begin with the prototype represented at (a) in figure 5.3. With minor alterations, this pattern represents the deepest level of structure of four of the movements of BWV 818a. At (b) we have a different pattern, an elaborated descent from scale-degree five, yet one that is related to (a). The primary difference between the two is the interpretation of f^2 and e^2. At (a) they are part of the fundamental line, but at (b) they are part of a lower-level descent introducing scale degree 4 of the fundamental line. The other difference, of course, is that a^2 is missing, and thus g^2 is interpreted as reaching above e^2 to introduce f^2 from above. Thus they are different, yet related. The

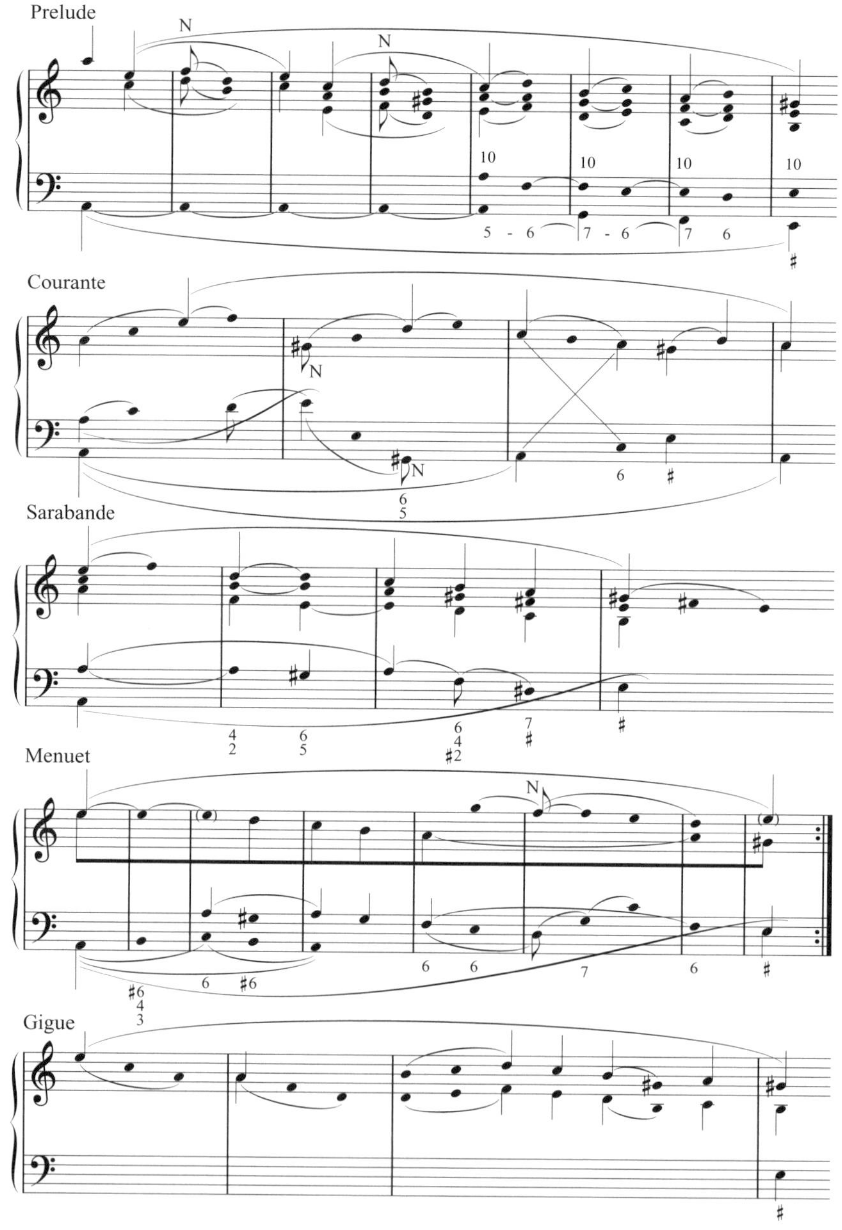

Figure 5.2. Interpretation of figure 5.1

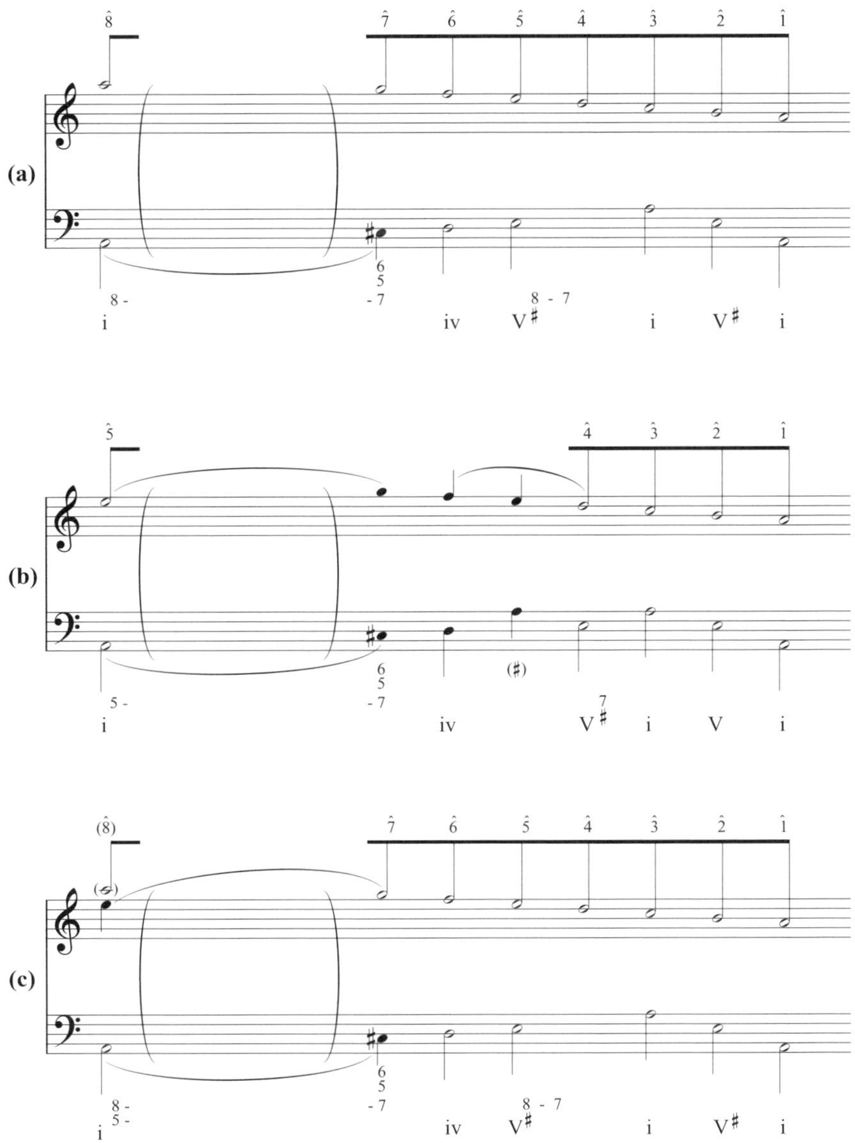

Figure 5.3. Structural models

relationship between the two becomes clearer when scale degrees 7 to 1 receive full harmonic support, as at (a). In this instance, the interpretation at (c), where a^2 ($\hat{8}$) is not stated but possibly implied by context, seems appropriate. This last type corresponds to the structures of the Sarabande simple from BWV 818 and of the Menuet from BWV 818a.

Prelude

The Prelude is divided into two large parts (bars 1–27 and 27–50)—marked by roman numerals in figure 5.4, a detailed sketch of the entire movement—followed by a coda (bars 50–58). This binary division is clearly articulated by the repetition of the opening material on the dominant, rearranged so that the third of the local tonic (g^2) is the highest sounding note, providing consonant support to that pitch as preparation for its later introduction as seventh of the dominant of the subdominant ($\hat{7}$ of the fundamental line). Though much has taken place in the interim, this g^2 (bar 38) is interpreted as associated at the deepest level with the opening a^2 ($\hat{8}$). From bar 38 the fundamental line begins its descent toward closure, which at the last minute is delayed by the deceptive motion and ensuing parenthetical statement (bars 45–49). The coda makes reference to the opening material, this time leading by arpeggiation to a^2, the opening pitch, before confirming closure in the lower octave.

The first part of the Prelude is subdivided into two large phrases, the first arriving at the cadence on III (bar 18) and the second at v (bar 27), creating a large-scale bass arpeggiation I–III–v. The first phrase opens with the neighbor-note figure on e^2, then on c^2, followed by a sequential progression leading to the dominant. This motion is contained within the larger motion to III, supporting an initial descent from the opening a^2 to c^2, a motion to an inner voice. The outer voice g^2 is implied at this point, then confirmed by subsequent events leading to the cadence in bar 27.

The deepest level of melodic motion is shown to be an octave progression, where g^2 is twice provided consonant support, first by III, then by v, before becoming a dissonant seventh, setting in motion the descent

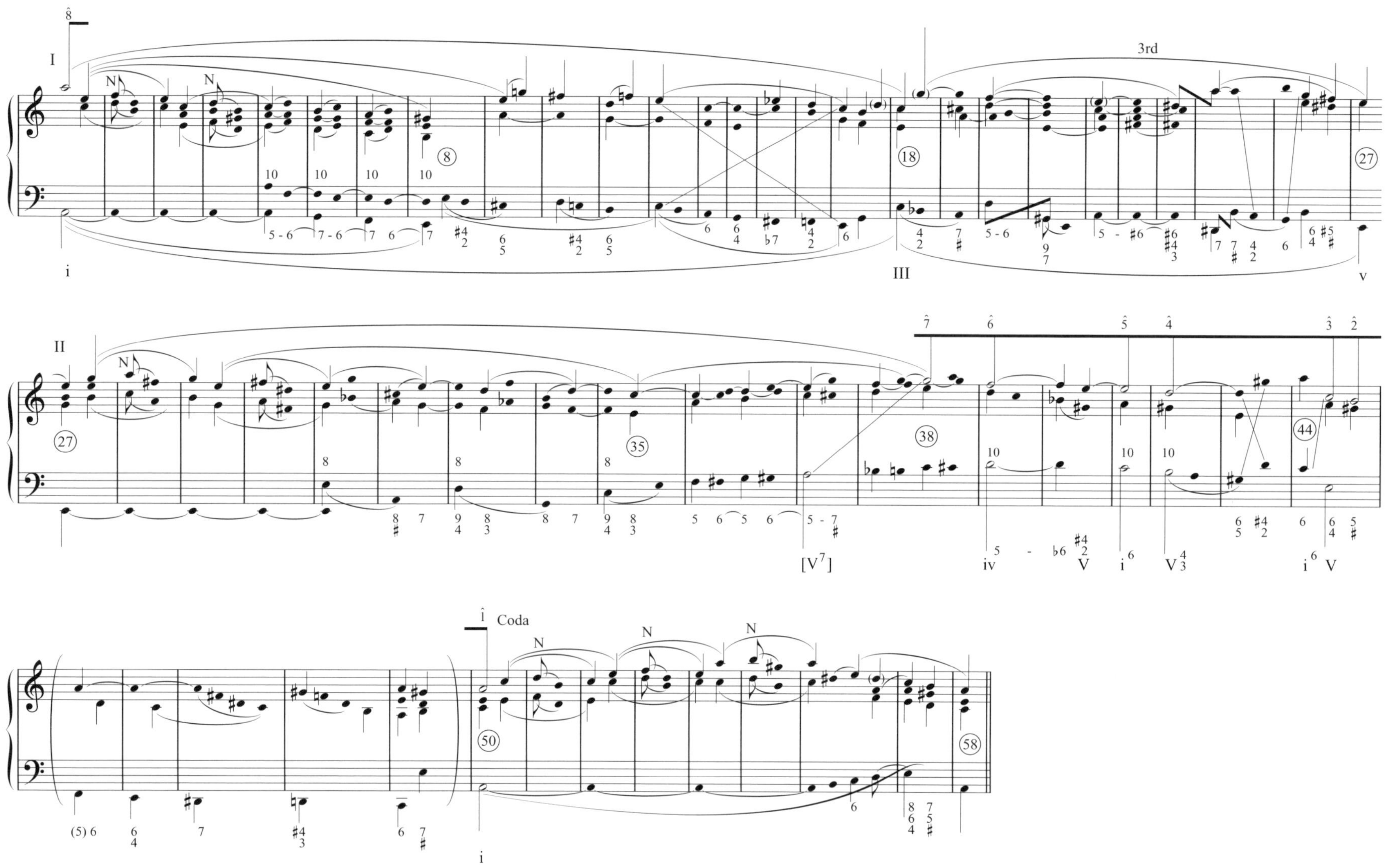

Figure 5.4. Prelude

Figure 5.5. Allemande

to closure. This is a pattern that is repeated in varied form in several other movements.

Allemande

The Allemande, though relatively short in length, is a sophisticated contrapuntal movement, not unlike some of the movements in the English and French Suites. As shown in figure 5.5, the first note of the fundamental line (a^2) is introduced in bar 2, following the opening idea, which bears a motivic resemblance to the other movements.[3] From this a^2 there is an initial descent of a fourth, a^2–g^2–$f\sharp^2$–e^2 over the course of the first part, a motion that prolongs the initiating tone ($\hat{8}$). This interpretation is based on hearing e^2 implied in bars 9–10 covering the continued descent to $g\sharp^1$ at the cadence on V.[4] In the second part a^2 is reinstated, supported by a D-minor, then D-major, harmony that is extended over several measures. This leads to a G-major harmony (VIII) providing consonant support to g^2 (bar 17) before that pitch is reintroduced in bar 19 as the dissonant seventh of the dominant of the subdominant, that is, as scale degree 7 of the fundamental line, from which point the line leads directly and convincingly to closure. A condensed version of the detailed sketch of the voice-leading is provided in figure 5.6. Here one can see quite easily the strong relationship between the Allemande and the Prelude at deeper structural levels.

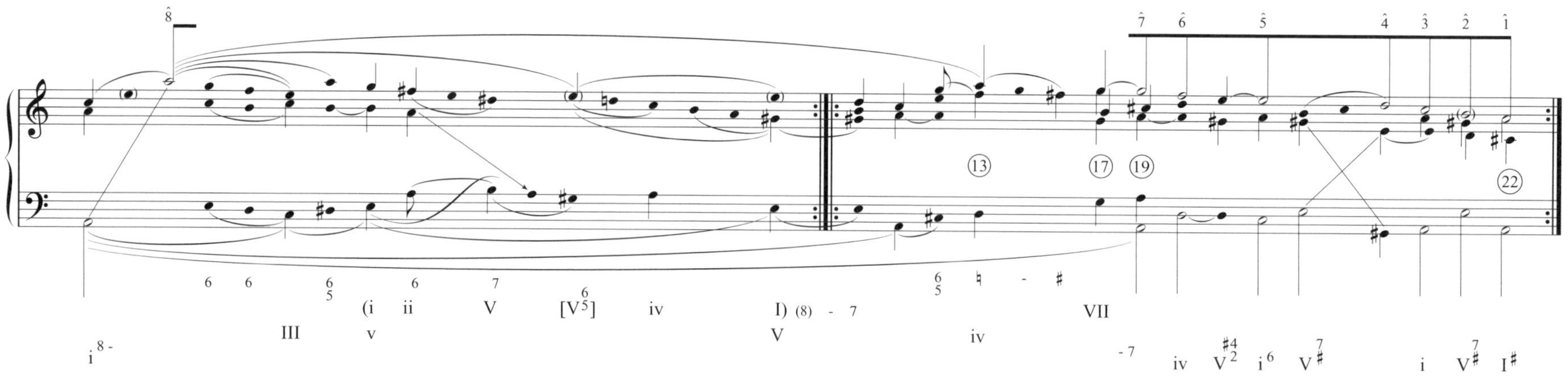

Figure 5.6. Allemande

Courante

The Courante is quite brief (only sixteen bars in length), suggesting the date of composition as much earlier than the French or English suites. Its voice-leading structure, shown in figure 5.7, bears strong resemblances to both the Prelude and the Allemande. As in the Allemande, the primary tone ($\hat{8}$) is introduced following the statement of an initial motivic idea, here a four-bar phrase. Following the introduction of a^2 the melodic line descends a fifth from g^2 to c^2, the latter coinciding with arrival at the cadence on III in bar 8. This motion is shown to prolong the initiating tone of the descent, and though g^2 is only implied in bar 8, it is immediately reinstated in the following phrase before descending through f♯² to e^2 at the cadence on the dominant in bar 12. To this point the overall tonal motion is I–III–v supporting an initial descent a^2–g^2–f♯²–e^2, exactly as occurred at this level in the first part of the Prelude. (Since the Prelude was written later, perhaps it would be more appropriate to say that the structure of its first part parallels bars 1–12 of the Courante). This large-scale motion is embedded within a larger tonic prolongation, where the initial tonic supporting $\hat{8}$is transformed into a major harmony supporting $\hat{7}$leading to $\hat{6}$supported by subdominant harmony and from there on to closure. Note that the support for scale degree 5 in this descent is harmonically "weak." The setting is, in fact, a contrapuntal one, with the outer voices progressing in parallel tenths, a feature that reappears in the final movement. In figure 5.8, a simplification of the more detailed sketch, harmonies are added in parenthesis at this point to show the correspondence to the equivalent passage in the Allemande.

Sarabande

While there are clear associations between the Sarabande and other movements in this suite, its deep-level structure differs. This movement is not controlled by an octave descent, but by a fifth, much like the prototype at (b) in figure 5.3. Figure 5.9 provides a sketch of this brief movement. Following the opening motion from outer to inner voice (from e^2 to g♯¹), the melodic line descends to c^2 at the cadence on III in bar 8. The primary tone, e^2, is reinstated at the outset of part 2 and prolonged through the cadence on the dominant in bar 16. Internal to this phrase, g^2 is introduced by its upper neighbor note and then descends through f♯² to e^2 at the cadence. This melodic motion g^2–f♯²–e^2 is very reminiscent of the same progression in the Prelude (bars 26–27) and in the

Figure 5.7. Courante

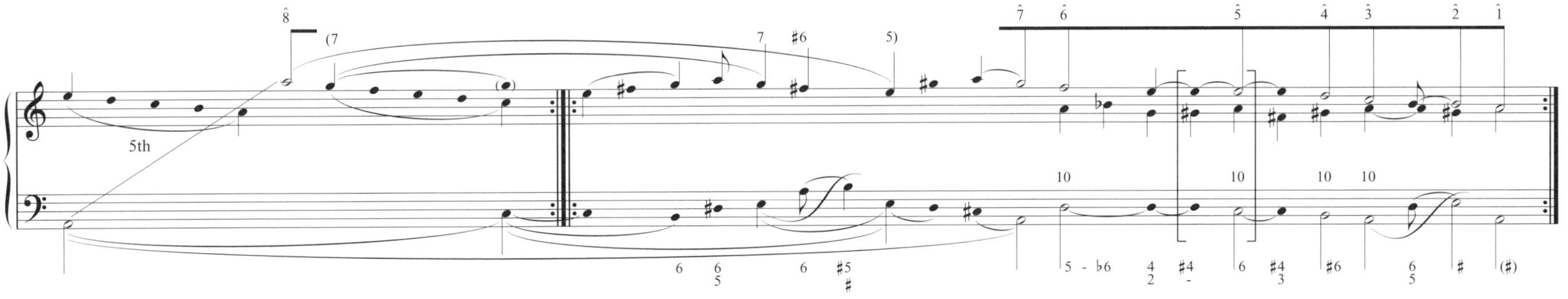

Figure 5.8. Courante

Figure 5.9. Sarabande

Courante (bars 11–12), less clearly in bars 6–10 of the Allemande. What is different is the chromatic harmonization of this progression, which anticipates but does not totally prepare the listener for the chromaticism of the inner voices in bars 18–19. The large-scale harmonic progression of bars 1–16 is the familiar arpeggiation i–III–v, and immediately following the cadence on v, f^2—supported by subdominant harmony—is introduced by the even more familiar secondary dominant seventh of iv with g^2 in the top voice and c♯ in the bass. Here, however, f^2 is not $\hat{6}$ in a fundamental descent, but the upper third of $\hat{4}$, which is harmonized as seventh of the dominant leading directly to $\hat{3}$ supported by tonic harmony in bar 19. Closure does not follow immediately, but is delayed as shown in figure 5.9, creating an eight-bar phrase to balance the earlier two phrases of that length.

Sarabande simple (BWV 818)

While the Sarabande from BWV 818a exhibits a fundamental structure akin to prototype (b) in figure 5.3, the structure of the original Sarabande appears to be a hybrid between prototypes (a) and (b), namely (c), an octave descent lacking the initial pitch (a^2).[5] There are two reasons for this interpretation, as opposed to a reading from $\hat{5}$. First, there is the considerable emphasis given to g^2. The introduction of g^2 in bar 5 and subsequent descent to c^2 at the cadence on III in bar 8 is not sufficient in itself to warrant this interpretation, since g^2 here can easily be explained as coming from e^2 in order to introduce f^2 from above. However, the conspicuous introduction of g^2 in bar 5 coupled with its later emphasis in bars 9–16 adds credence to this interpretation, though

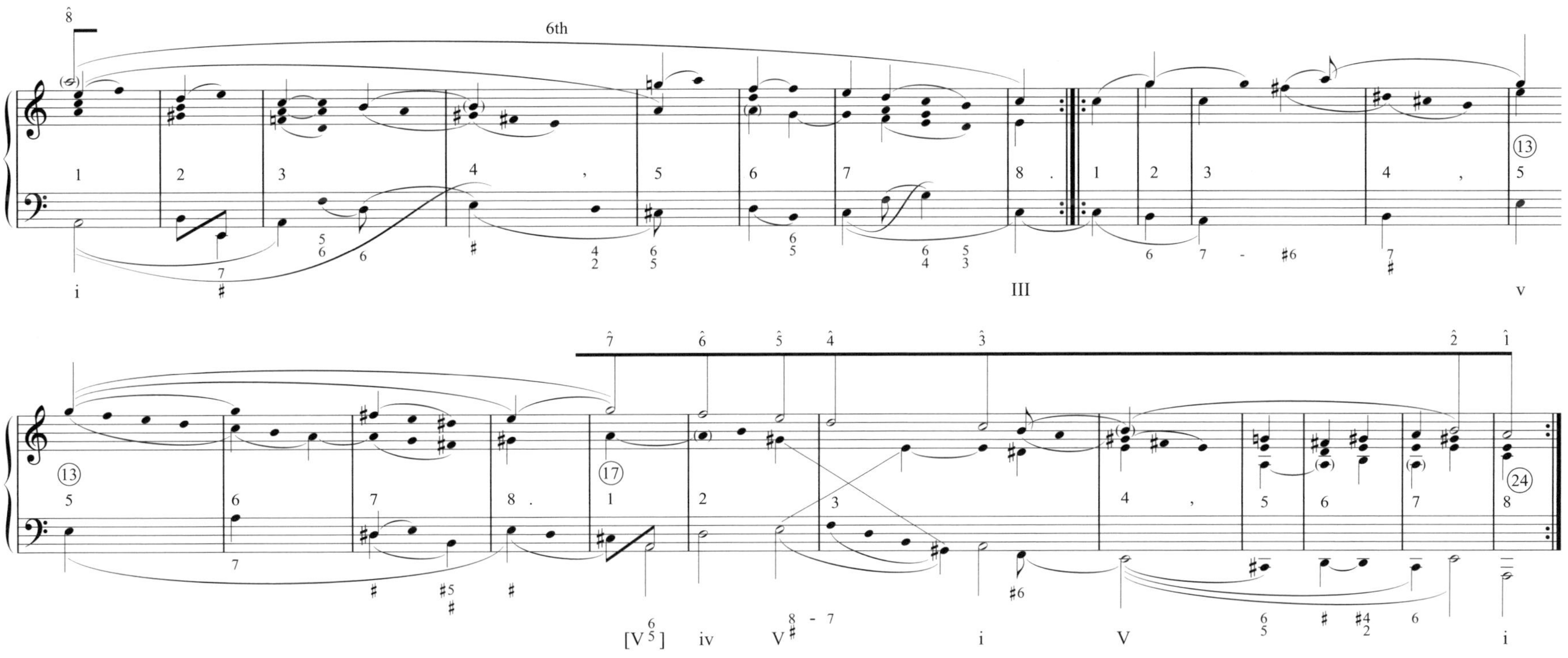

Figure 5.10. Sarabande simple (BWV 818)

it would still be possible to hear g^2 as the upper third of e^2. The clincher comes in the final eight bars where there is a fully harmonized descent from scale degree 7 to closure on the tonic, unlike the equivalent passage in the later version, where scale degree 5 receives no support. An interpretation of the voice-leading of the Sarabande simple from BWV 818 is provided in figure 5.10.

Menuet

The main reason for including the earlier version of the Sarabande in our brief examination of BWV 818a is that its structure—an octave descent a^2–a^1 lacking the initial pitch—occurs in modified form in both the Menuet and in the Gigue. Like the Sarabande, the Menuet opens emphatically from e^2 (scale degree 5), and from there the line descends a sixth to $g\sharp^1$ at the half-cadence in bar 8. This motion to an inner voice is covered by another line generated from g^2 in bar 5 leading to an implied e^2 at the cadence. Though this upper line is shown in figure 5.11 as originating from an implied a^2 in the very beginning, there is no compelling reason at this point to hear this first phrase as anything but a prolongation of $\hat{5}$. Those reasons come later. In any case, no matter how we interpret the events of part 1, the motion initiated in those opening bars continues into part 2 with the upper line continuing its descent through d^2 to c^2 and the inner voice $g\sharp^1$ resolving to a^1 over

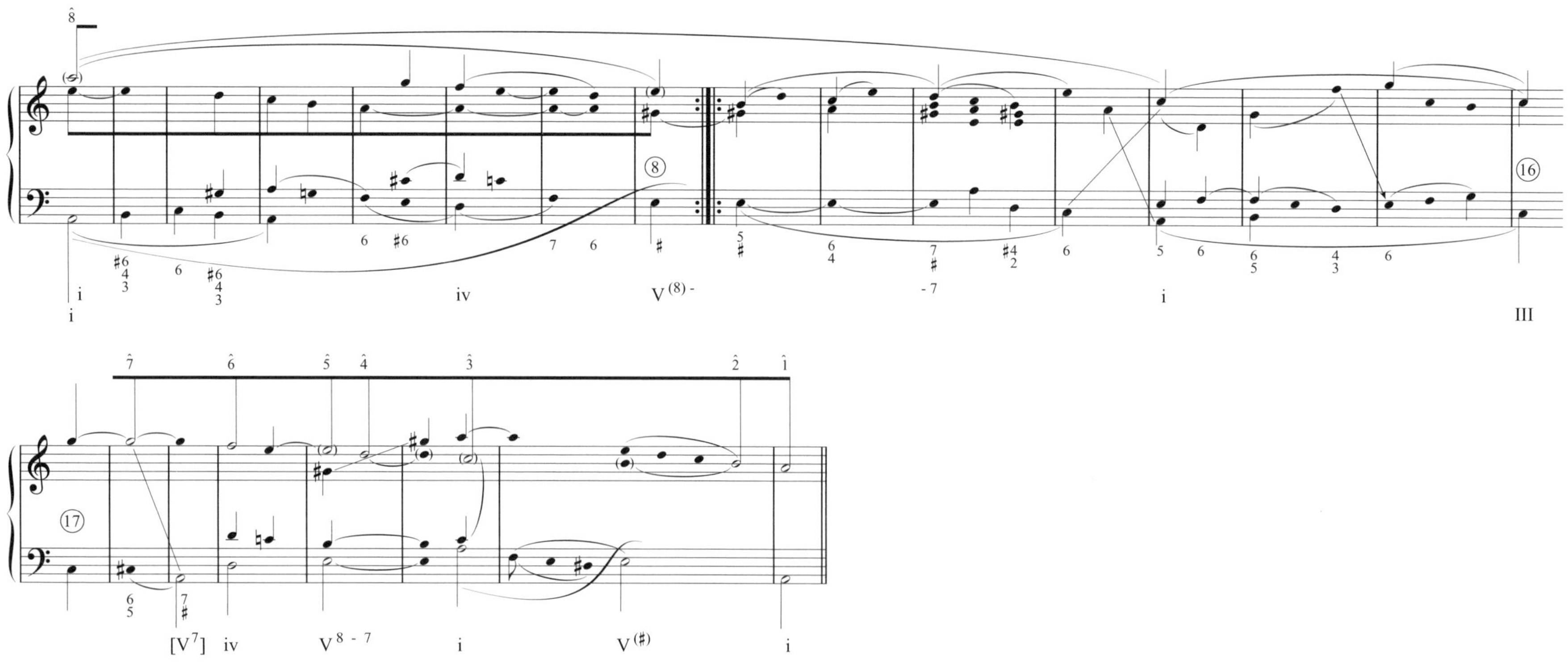

Figure 5.11. Menuet

tonic harmony in bars 12–13. This motion is embedded within a larger connection between the initial tonic and the cadence on III in bar 16. This is followed immediately by the emphatic articulation of g^2 in bars 17–18, initially receiving consonant support as the fifth of a C-major harmony and then as the now familiar dissonant seventh of the dominant of iv with c♯ in the bass, that is, as scale degree 7 in a larger octave descent. From this point the line descends, fully harmonized, to closure, similar to what we have heard in four of the five movements discussed so far. It is the strong articulation of g^2 and the subsequent descent from there which binds this movement so closely to others in this suite and ultimately which suggests the interpretation presented here.

Gigue

As noted above the Gigue exhibits a fundamental structure related both to the Menuet and the original Sarabande, namely, an octave descent with its initial pitch (a^2) implied but not stated. The first part exhibits a large-scale harmonic motion we have heard several times before: i–III (bar 18)–V (bar 24). This in itself is not remarkable, but gains in potential significance when we recognize that the melodic motion it supports is a compound version of the descending fourth a–g–f♯–e heard previously in the Prelude (bars 1–27) and in the Courante (bars 1–12) in conjunction with the same progression. Here the fourth is an eleventh, divided into two descending sixths, (a^2)–c^2 and c^2–e^1, the point of

Figure 5.12. Gigue

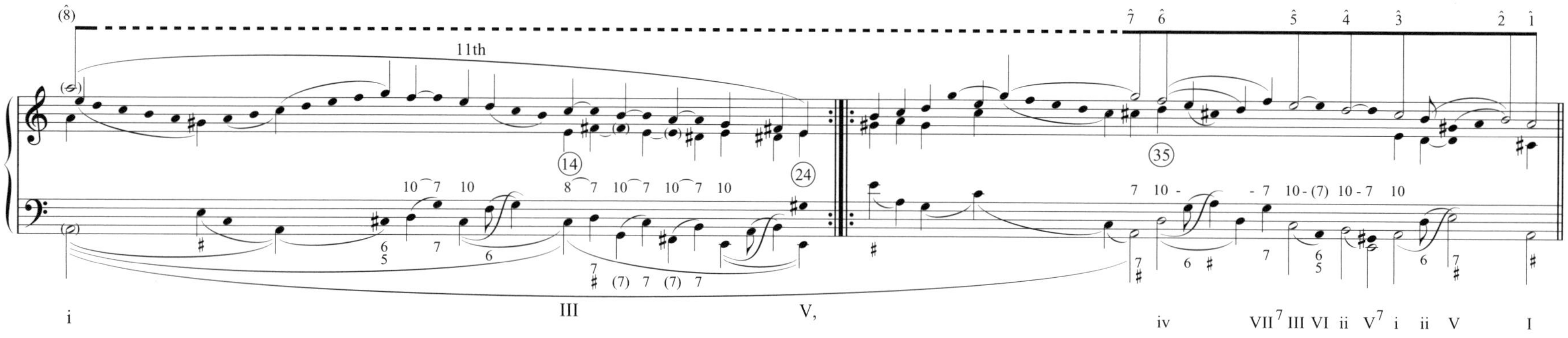

Figure 5.13. Gigue

division being articulated by the cadence on III (bar 18). See figure 5.12, which provides a detailed account of the voice-leading of the entire movement. The motion to V in part one prolongs the initial tonic and, as indicated by the comma following roman numeral V in the sketch at bar 24, this prolongation is embedded within a larger-scale motion from initial tonic to III supporting g^2 (bar 29), which is subsequently prolonged by a descending fifth to c^2 supported by the cadence on III in bar 33. Once again we find consonant support for g^2 in preparation for its harmonization as a dissonant seventh of the major tonic chord, namely as $\hat{7}$ in the fundamental line, leading to f^2 ($\hat{6}$) supported by the subdominant in bar 35. Unlike the earlier movements, the continuing descent to closure is not immediate. First $\hat{6}$ and the subdominant harmony are prolonged through bar 39, internal to which there is a descent of a third: f^2–e^2–d^2. The harmonic progression generated from bar 35 is a sequence by descending fifths from iv to i, one consequence of which is the contrapuntal setting in parallel tenths between top voice and bass for the structural descent as far as $\hat{3}$, after which the line continues to closure supported by a standard cadential progression. A condensed sketch of the movement is provided in figure 5.13.

BWV 818a is a highly unified work motivically and with respect to large-scale harmonic-structural associations. The motivic parallels—the different manifestations of the common pitch motive noted in figure 5.1 as well as the related voice-leading patterns in figure 5.2—are very clearly audible to the trained ear, despite the differences in surface design of the various movements. Less obvious, perhaps, are the large-scale voice-leading associations, the identical and near-identical background structures. In this respect, we have put quite a bit of effort into the preceding paragraphs addressing rather fine points of interpretation of background structure. These matters are of considerable concern to those interested in structural analysis and theory. Indeed there are important differences among the three prototypes listed in figure 5.3, but it is also true that the three, particularly (a) and (c), are very closely related, and it is the commonality that is most relevant to this study. With the exception of the Sarabande, the movements of this suite exhibit very similar structures involving the descent of an octave, in three instances $\hat{8}$ implied but not stated. This is remarkable, particularly in light of the unanimity of harmonic support for $\hat{8}$–$\hat{7}$–$\hat{6}$ namely i . . . [V^7] iv, as revealed in figure 5.14. In fact, the six-five harmony on c♯ is so prevalent in this work that it almost assumes motivic status. In all cases g^2 ($\hat{7}$) is provided consonant support in preparation for its introduction as a dissonant seventh, a trigger, it seems, to initiate the descent toward closure. Also contributing to our perception of unity in this work are repeated patterns at the middleground level, for example, the descent a^2–g^2–f♯^{2}–e^2 in conjunction with the harmonic motion i–III–V and the descent of the fifth g^2–c^2 at various levels within passages controlled by III.

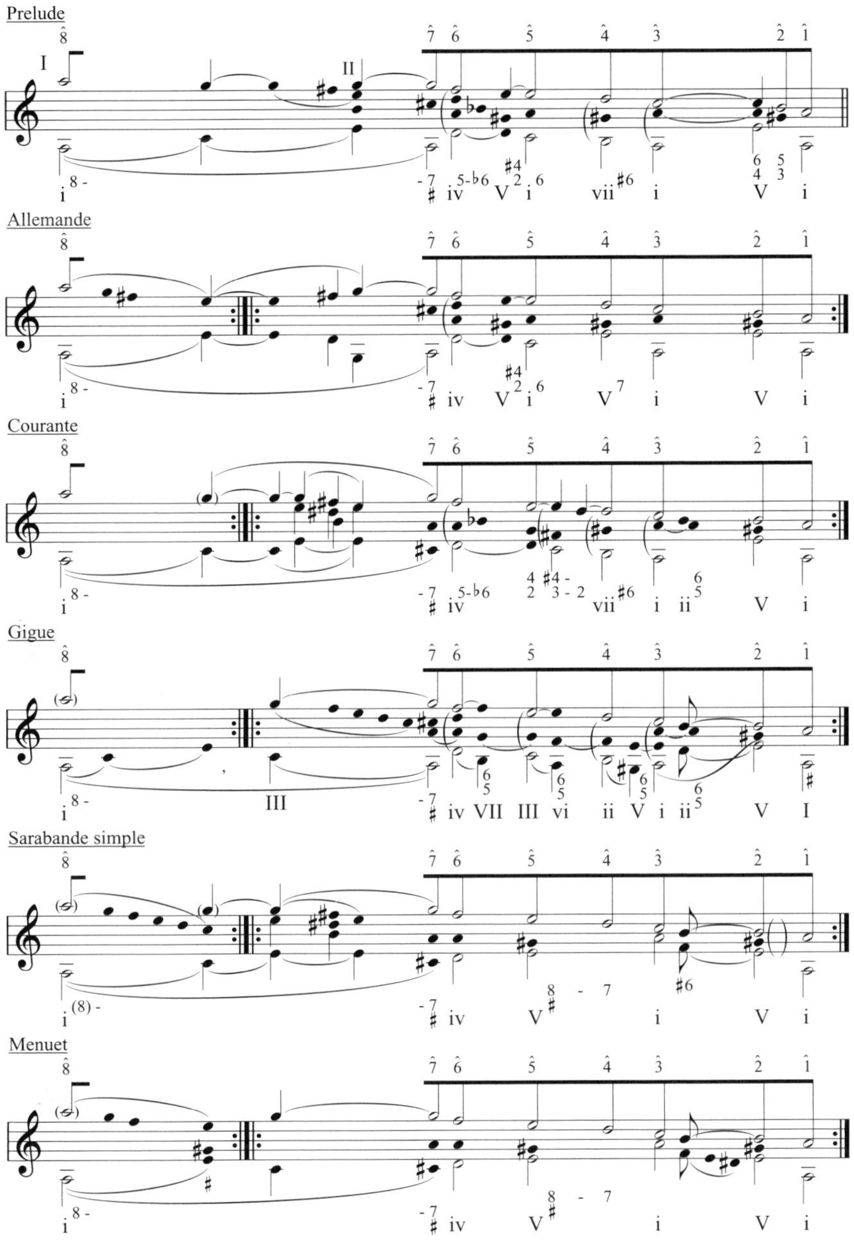

Figure 5.14. Comparison of structures

Notes

1. David Schulenberg, *The Keyboard Music of J. S. Bach* (New York: Schirmer, 1992), 257.

2. In *Free Composition*, Schenker provides a prototype of the octave descent of the *Urlinie* in the major mode (see his figure 11) and places on it the restriction that the seventh degree of the scale must be natural, not lowered, as one frequently finds in codas (p. 21). No prototype is given for such a descent in the minor mode, though logic dictates that the natural progression would be the descending form of the scale. This is confirmed by Schenker's reading of two of the Short Preludes by Bach, numbers 6 (BWV 940) and 12 (BWV 942) in *Das Meisterwerk in der Musik* I (1925), both translated by Hedi Siegel and published in *The Masterwork in Music* I, ed. William Drabkin, 54–57 and 62–66, respectively (Cambridge: Cambridge University Press, 1994).

3. The motivic association to the other movements is not explicit, but rather implied by the incomplete neighbor note f^2.

4. BWV 818 has $d\natural^2$ rather than $d\sharp^2$ as the final sounding melodic note in bar 8, weakening the effect of that pitch in the following bar. The subsequent change to $d\sharp^2$ at this point strengthens the hearing of the later $d\natural^2$ as a substitute for the expected e^2, a common device employed by Bach at final cadences.

5. The Sarabande from the French Suite in E Major (BWV 817) is also interpreted as controlled by an octave descent missing the initial pitch ($\hat{8}$). See chapter 6, pp. 77–78.

6

French Suite VI in E Major (BWV 817)

CIRCUMSTANCES SURROUNDING THE COMPOSITION of the last of the French Suites are not known, though it seems likely that it was written around 1725, somewhat later than the early versions of the first five, which are contained in the *Clavierbüchlein for Anna Magdalena Bach* (1722–25). The Urtext of the New Bach Edition presents us with two versions of the six, one based on a copy in the hand of Bach's student and son-in-law, Johann Christoph Altnickol, and a second one assembled from various later sources, including a manuscript in the hand of another Bach student, Heinrich Nicolas Gerber. An intriguing feature of the Gerber version of the last suite is the inclusion of the Prelude in E Major (BWV 854/1) from *The Well-Tempered Clavier I,*[1] suggesting that Bach might originally have intended this work to be one of the suites with preludes. Unless further documentation is uncovered, the reason for Gerber's inclusion of the Prelude will remain speculative, though it seems likely that the idea must have originated with the composer. Perhaps Gerber heard Bach play the suite that way. Consider the following description of the elder Gerber's studies published by his son some years later in his *Lexicon der Tonkünstler.*[2]

> At the first lesson he (Bach) set his Inventions before him. When he had studied these through to Bach's satisfaction, there followed a series of suites, then *The Well-Tempered Clavier.* This latter work Bach played altogether three times through for him with his unmatchable art, and my father counted these among his happiest hours, when Bach, under the pretext of not feeling in the mood to teach, sat himself at one of his fine instruments and thus turned these hours into minutes.[3]

This account does not say that Bach played the suites for his student, only the *Well-Tempered Clavier,* though it is not much of a stretch of the imagination to suppose that he might have done so. In any case we do know from this quote that he had the elder Gerber study a series of suites somewhere along the way, and it must have been through those studies that he encountered the E-major suite in this fashion. As it turns out the best evidence we have is the music itself. Careful examination of the Prelude reveals compelling evidence of strong compositional links between it and the suite, particularly the opening movements, and thus we will begin with a close look at the Prelude (BWV 854/1). Our investigation of the suite proper will be divided into two parts: first, the Standard Movements (Allemande, Courante, Sarabande, and Gigue), which are motivically and structurally related amongst themselves and to the Prelude; and second, the Optional Movements (Gavotte, Polonaise, Menuet, and Bourrée), which exhibit a different set of relationships amongst themselves, yet with occasional seeming references to the other movements.

Prelude

The Prelude is divided into three clear phrases, marked A, B, and A^1 in figure 6.1, a detailed account of the voice-leading structure of this movement.[4] The first phrase (bars 1–8) modulates to the dominant, and the second phrase, which begins from the cadence on the dominant, functions as a transition, leading to a varied repetition of the opening phrase beginning from the subdominant (bars 15–24).[5] An important motive, one that helps to articulate the deep-level structure of this work, is the arpeggiation figure, repetitions of which are highlighted in figure 6.1 by brackets. The first three statements of this idea articulate the large-scale arpeggiation e^2 (bar 1)–$g\sharp^2$ (bar 3)–b^2 (bar 9), the primary tone, which is reached only after the modulation to the dominant is achieved. The later arpeggiation to scale degree 4 (a^2) in bar 15, supported by subdominant harmony, connects registrally and motivically to the earlier motion to b^2 ($\hat{5}$). Another important feature is the prominent d♮ in bar 11, which anticipates the later d♮ in bar 14. These features—the large-scale arpeggiation to scale degree 5, the prominent use of d♮, and the registral connection of the b^2 in bar 9 to the a^2 in bar 15, as well as the subsequent registral isolation of those two pitches—are important characteristics of this piece. And, as we shall see, they are compositional features which link this Prelude to the suite.

Figure 6.1. Prelude in E (BWV 854/1)

Let us turn our attention to details of the voice-leading, beginning with the first phrase. The first part of the large-scale arpeggiation to b^{2}, that is, the connection between e^{2} and g♯^{2}, is easy to hear. From the g♯^{2} in bar 3 there is a descent of a sixth to b^{1} at the cadence in bar 8, which is then followed by the surface arpeggiation to the upper register, thus completing the long-range arpeggiation to $\hat{5}$. The voice-leading of the descending sixth is complex. First g♯^{2} is prolonged by a descent to the inner voice tone c♯^{2} over a prolonged e in the bass supporting the common voice-leading motion 5–6. This is followed by a second descent to the inner voice, this time from f♯^{2}, within the prolonged dominant of the new key (V). The prominent use of the chromatic d♮ in the descent to the inner voice foreshadows the use of that pitch later in the Prelude. As shown in figure 6.1, this preliminary descent from f♯^{2} (bars 5–7) is embedded within the longer-range descent to b^{1} at the cadence. This gesture, the descent from f♯^{2} to c♯^{2} in bars 5–7, is followed by a chromatic line leading from g♮^{2} to b^{1}, a summary of the larger gesture at its conclusion. One consequence of the chromatic writing is the displacement of pitches in the structural descent in relation to their supporting harmonies. As indicated by the diagonal line in the sketch, the e^{2} sounded on the downbeat of bar 8 can be understood to belong with the F♯ harmony of the preceding bar, and this e^{2} momentarily displaces the following d♯^{2} supported by the local tonic (B).

The voice-leading of phrase 2, the connecting phrase, is no less complex. As already noted, the deepest-level melodic connection is b^{2} (bar 9) to a^{2} at the beginning of the third phrase. The b^{2} is prolonged at the largest level by a descending third in which the passing tone a is first supported by a consonant harmony, that is, by an F♯-minor chord, before being harmonized as the seventh of the prolonged dominant harmony. This seventh resolves as expected to the g♯ over tonic harmony, which, with the addition of the d♮, leads us to the subdominant. At a more immediate level the prolonged b is destabilized, becoming the seventh of the secondary dominant chord on c♯, which is extended through bar 12 and involves a transfer to the lower register before its resolution over the F♯-minor harmony on the downbeat of bar 13. Internal to this complex passage is the introduction of the d♮ as 9th of this secondary dominant (more locally as the seventh of the secondary diminished-seventh chord).

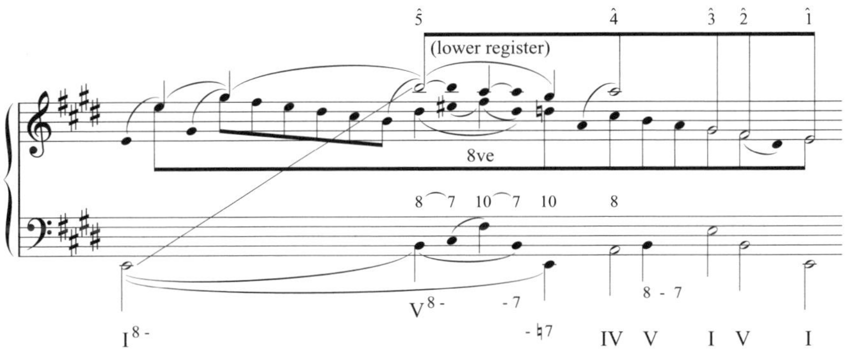

Figure 6.2. Prelude in E (BWV 854/1)

The final phrase is a duplication of the initial phrase transposed to the subdominant. However, there are two important changes. The first involves a shift to the lower register. Instead of arpeggiation from the c♯^{2} on the downbeat of bar 17 up to c♯^{3} as might be expected, Bach rewrites to remain on c♯^{2}, from which the phrase progresses to closure in this lower register. The second change involves the avoidance of closure in the second half of bar 22 and the subsequent extension of the phrase by two bars. This is a common procedure in Bach's instrumental music, one that is repeated at the close of the Courante and Bourrée movements from the E-major French Suite.

An overview of the deep structure of the Prelude is provided in figure 6.2. There are three important points to be made here. First note that the arpeggiation to scale degree 5 and the subsequent motion from it are superimposed on the descent of an octave spanning the entire piece. This octave is generated from the e^{2} in bar 1, which progresses through the dividing dominant at the cadence in bar 8 to the tonic harmony with lowered seventh (d♮) in bar 14 as V^{7} of IV. From bar 15 the line descends a sixth from c♯^{2} to e^{1}, the parallel to the descending sixth within the initial phrase. Second, let us examine the harmonic progression supporting this octave descent. As shown by the bass and roman numerals, the modulation to the dominant and its subsequent extension are embedded within a tonic prolongation supporting the motion 8–♮7 (e^{2} to d♮^{2}), thus uniting the two phrases. Finally, it is important to comment on the unusual registral distribution of the fundamental line. We have already noted the registral isolation of the b^2 in bar 9 and the a^2 of bar 15, scale degrees 5 and 4 of the fundamental line. Because of the registral shift in bar 17, completion of the fundamental line occurs in the lower register in conjunction with the completion of the inner voice octave descent. It is almost as if the upper part is never completed properly, at least registrally. It is interesting that Bach chose to end the subsequent fugue (*Well-Tempered Clavier I*) in the upper register, thus completing a registral connection unrealized in the Prelude.

I. The Standard Movements

Allemande

Voice-leading sketches of the Allemande are provided in figures 6.3 (details) and 6.4 (overview).[6] The connection between the Allmenade and the Prelude is immediately apparent in the opening four bars of the suite movement. As indicated in figure 6.3, the features of this phrase that exist just below the surface mimic the overall structure of the Prelude. The main melodic gesture is an arpeggiation to scale degree 5, e^2–$g\sharp^2$–b^2, followed by a stepwise descent back to e^2. Less obvious is the inner voice descent of the octave e^2–e^1 indicated in the sketch. More careful examination reveals even closer similarities. Note that arrival at b^2 in bar 2 occurs over the dominant harmony, as occurred in the Prelude. The difference is one of level: in the Prelude, arrival at b^2 occurs after modulation to the dominant, while here it occurs in conjunction with a local change to that harmony. Immediately following this point in the Allemande (bar 2, beat 3), d♮ is introduced in an inner voice in conjunction with a return to the tonic harmony, just as we found in the approach to the third phrase in the Prelude, directing the motion to a^2 over $c\sharp^2$ supported by subdominant harmony, from which point the phrase progresses to local closure. Thus all the main features of the Prelude are encapsulated in these four bars. But there is an important distinction. Here the arpeggiation from e^2 to b^2 and the return to e^2 is heard within a local prolongation of the tonic (a closed phrase). The controlling pitch is e^2 (scale degree 8) and it is from this pitch that the fundamental line progresses.

As shown in figure 6.3, the melodic line descends from the e^2 in bar 4, first as far as $c\sharp^2$ on the downbeat of bar 7, but that progression turns out to be a motion to an inner voice. The e^2 is still active, finally giving way to $d\sharp^2$–$c\sharp^2$–b^1 (scale degrees 7–6–5 of the fundamental line) at the cadence in bar 8. In the following extension of the cadence the upper line progresses to the high b, picking up the b^2 of bar 2 and setting up the continuation, while the lower line remains anchored on b^1, scale degree 5 of the fundamental line.[7] It is important as we move into part 2 of the Allemande, where the voice-leading is more difficult to interpret, to keep in mind that the primary register is the lower one and that the b^2, from which the second part proceeds, is covering.

The complex voice-leading of part 2 is most easily explained beginning with the large picture and within that context considering greater detail. As indicated in figure 6.3, tonal closure is achieved on the downbeat of bar 25, and the major point of articulation prior to that is the cadence on c♯ in bar 20. Figure 6.4 shows that the function of the c♯ in the bass is passing within a prolonged dominant, that is, as a passing tone between the root and third of the dominant, supporting the motion 8–7 (scale degrees 5 and 4 of the fundamental line), from which point the line proceeds to immediate closure, completing the descent of the octave e^2 to e^1. This octave descent is interpreted as fundamental and the arpeggiation to b^2 and its continuation as covering, the opposite of our interpretation of those elements in the Prelude. This is a subtle though significant distinction for those interested in structural analysis.[8] However, within this context, the most important point is that the basic elements, the octave descent and the arpeggiation to b^2 as well as its continuation, are the same in these two movements.

Returning now to the details of the voice-leading, let us look at what leads to the cadence on c♯ (bar 20), keeping in mind that the high b^2 from which the second part begins is covering; the primary register is below in the inner voice. Beginning in bar 13, the top sounding line descends by step as far as $c\sharp^2$ in bar 16, above which the high a^2 is introduced. Registrally, we hear a link between the b^2 of bar 13 and the a^2 of bar 16, just as we hear $c\sharp^2$, the goal of the descending motion, as connected to the b^1 of bar 12. The $c\sharp^2$ is introduced by d♮, an element that takes on greater prominence in the following bar, where we hear it as the lowered second scale degree in relation to the goal of this motion, the cadence on c♯. Though the harmonies are different, the parallel with the Prelude is striking. Meanwhile, the top sounding part (now on a^2) begins to descend

Figure 6.3. Allemande

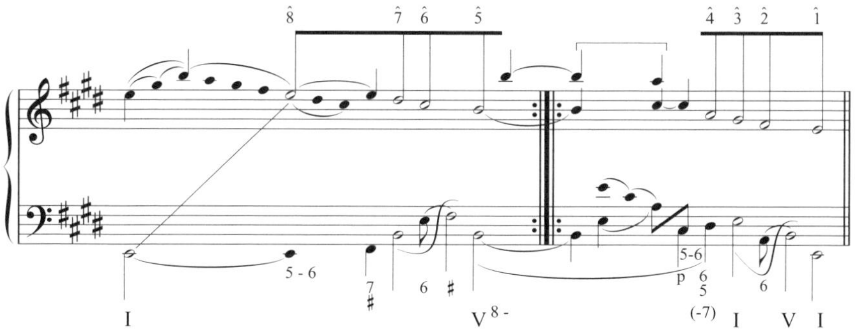

Figure 6.4. Allemande

once again by step, finally reaching the c♯ in bar 20. The descents, first from b² and then from a², bring attention to these two pitches, and the continuation only in the lower register from the c♯ cadence to the point of closure leaves them registrally isolated. The purpose of the bracket above these pitches in figure 6.4 is to highlight this prominent feature of the Allemande, another feature it has in common with the Prelude.

The passage connecting the cadence on c♯ (bar 20) and the completion of the fundamental line (the octave) in bars 24–25 involves local prolongation of c♯², first by a stepwise motion down to a¹ and then an ascent back to c♯², from which point the line skips to a¹ ($\hat{4}$) on the downbeat of bar 24. As shown in figure 6.4, this c♯, which receives consonant support, functions as a kind of harmonized escape tone in relation to the longer-range connection between scale degrees 5 and 4 of the fundamental line.

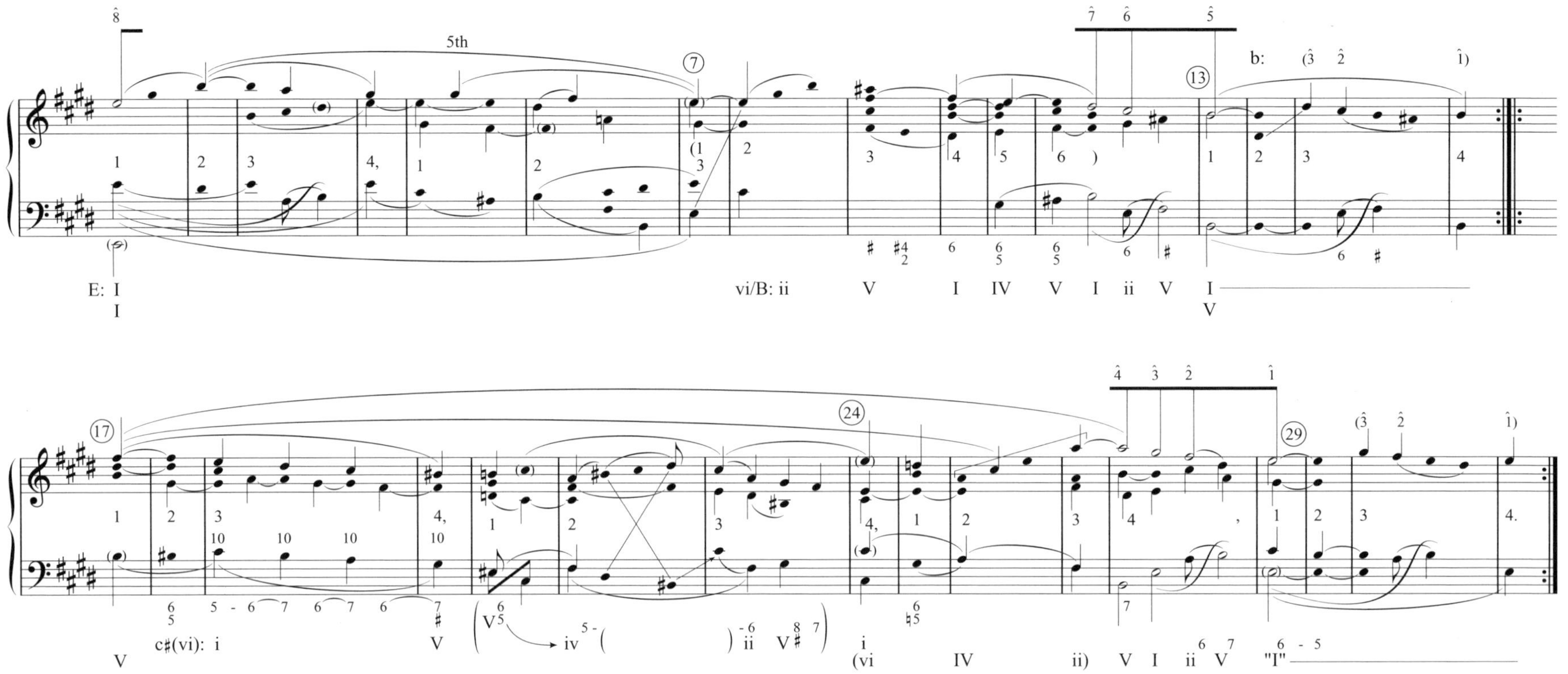

Figure 6.5. Courante

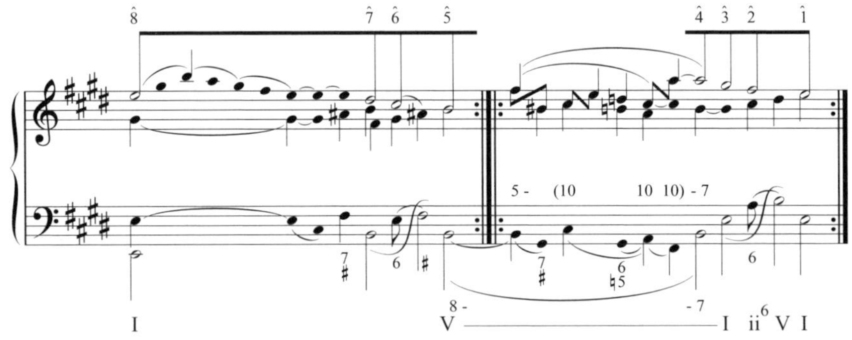

Figure 6.6. Courante

In closing our examination of this movement, I would like to summarize the features that it shares with the Prelude: the arpeggiation to b², the octave descent from e² to e¹ spanning each work; the registrally isolated b² and a²; and the prominent d♮. These two movements share these compositional features and in this sense they are linked. The Allemande is also structurally related to the other movements in this group: the Courante, the Sarabande, and the Gigue. All share the same fundamental line, the octave.

Courante

The Courante has an entirely different character than the Allemande, yet references to it and apparently to the Prelude as well are unmistakable.

The elements common to both these movements are all here: the arpeggiation to b^2, the octave descent, and the prominent $d\natural$. Sketches of the Courante are provided in figures 6.5 (detail) and 6.6 (overview).[9] As shown in figure 6.6, the fundamental line is an octave descent, as in the Allemande. The difference between the two is that here the descent involves transfer to and completion in the upper register, a feature of the Sarabande and Gigue as well. This transfer is accomplished by means of an arpeggiation to a^2 in bars 26–27, an unexpected gesture that, in light of the Gerber copy, would seem to be a direct reference to the arpeggiation motive of the later discarded Prelude. (This gesture is highlighted by a bracket in figure 6.5.) Upon attaining a^2 in bar 27, the top sounding part progresses almost immediately to closure in the upper register, only to be delayed at the last minute by the substitution in the bass of $c\sharp$ for the expected e.[10]

The Courante opens with the arpeggiation e^2–$g\sharp^2$–b^2, the last element of which is supported by a dominant harmony, as occurred in the Allemande and, at a much deeper level, in the Prelude. The stepwise descent back to the e^2 occurs in two stages, first a descent to $g\sharp^2$ in bar 4 and then by implication a return to e^2 in bar 7, over tonic harmony. The implied e^2 is stated on the downbeat of the following bar. Bar 7 is heard both as a point of arrival and as a point of departure, that is, as a point of metric reinterpretation. As indicated by the arabic numerals between the staves, the hypermeter, which elsewhere in the movement is quadruple, is irregular in these bars. As was the case with the opening phrase of the Allemande, the arpeggiation to b^2 and return to e^2 is heard within a local prolongation of the tonic, and it is from the e^2 in bar 8 that the fundamental line descends, reaching the local goal, scale degree 5, on the downbeat of bar 13.

As shown in figure 6.5, the second part opens with a four-bar phrase leading to the dominant of $c\sharp$ (vi). One might expect the melodic unfolding from $f\sharp^2$–$b\sharp^1$ spanning this phrase to be answered by $c\sharp^2$–e^2, supported by a $c\sharp$ harmony, as shown in figure 6.6. Instead, Bach cancels the $b\sharp$, redirecting the harmony temporarily to the subdominant of the goal harmony, which is reached in bar 24 after reintroduction of its dominant. (Note the introduction of $d\natural$ in bar 21 as ninth of the dominant of the following F♯-minor harmony). One consequence of this unexpected change is the continued descent of the melodic line, reaching its goal, e^1, in bar 24. However, the continuation occurs in the upper register with the introduction of $d\natural^2$ leading to $c\sharp^2$ supported by the subdominant harmony, completing a descending fourth from $f\sharp^2$ (bar 17) to $c\sharp^2$ (bar 26). It is at this point that a^2 is introduced by means of the arpeggiation figure, a seeming reference to that important gesture in the Prelude, as the bass completes its local descending arpeggiation to the supertonic harmony, which provides consonant support for the a^2 as preparation for its introduction as seventh of the prolonged dominant. As shown in figure 6.6, the arpeggiation from $f\sharp^2$ to a^2 (5–7 over the prolonged dominant) is embedded within a larger motion 8–7, that is, scale degrees 5 and 4 of the fundamental line.

Sarabande

Figure 6.7, a sketch of the Sarabande, provides an interpretation of the fundamental line as an octave descent with a transfer in the second part to the upper register, similar to what happens in the Courante. However, unlike the Courante, the descent does not originate from a clearly articulated e^2 supported by tonic harmony. Instead the melodic line ascends by step from the inner voice tone $g\sharp^1$ to the outer voice tone $d\sharp^2$, scale degree 7 of the fundamental line, in bar 6. Immediately preceding this point, e^2 as the seventh of the secondary dominant, is overlapped above $c\sharp^2$, thus approaching $d\sharp^2$ from above. As shown in figure 6.7, this e^2 in bar 6 may, in retrospect, be considered as connected conceptually to an implied stable e^2 associated with the opening tonic harmony.[11] The situation here is analogous to what we observed in the previous chapter regarding the fundamental structures of the Sarabande simple from BWV 818 (see figure 5.10, p. 65) and the Menuet and Gigue movements from BWV 818a (see figures 5.11 (p. 66) and 5.12/5.13 (p. 67–68), respectively), three different representations of the prototype given at c in figure 5.3 (p. 59).

Interpretation of the levels of voice-leading in part 2 presents particular challenges because of the nature of the embedding. At the largest level the dominant is shown to be prolonged from the cadence in bar 8 until its resolution to the tonic supporting scale degree 3 in the penultimate bar. That is, at the deepest level the motion is 8–7 over a prolonged

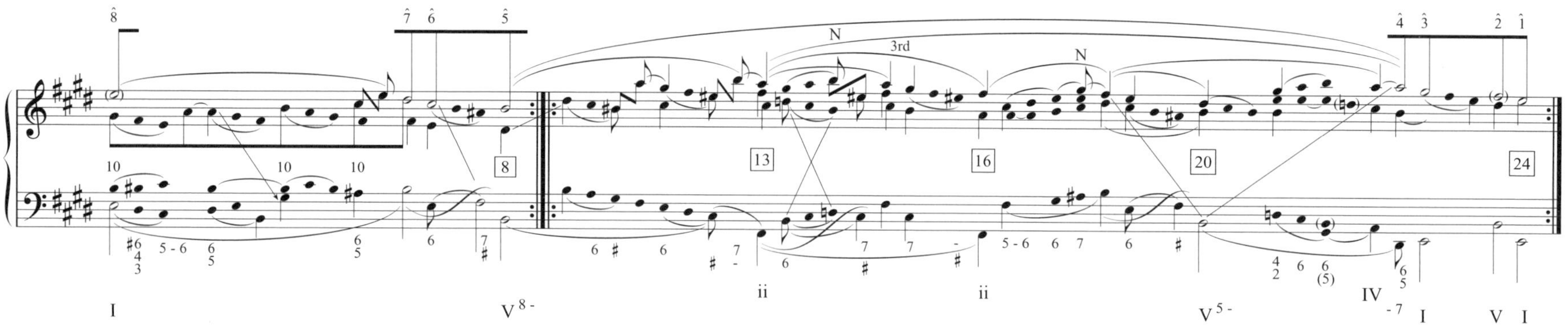

Figure 6.7. Sarabande

dominant, followed immediately by closure. Internal to this prolongation, a^2 is provided constant support in bar 13 and then prolonged by a descending third to the cadence on F♯ (supertonic) in bar 16. The next point of articulation is the reintroduction of the dominant in bar 20 following a further descending third in the top voice: $f\sharp^2 - e^2 - d\sharp^2$. In essence what we have is an unfolding from the outer voice tone a^2, supported by supertonic harmony, to $d\sharp^2$, supported by a return to the dominant. By implication a^2 has now become a dissonance, and we might expect direct introduction of a^2 at this point. Eventually a^2 is reintroduced as seventh of the dominant, but first it is introduced as a consonance, supported by the subdominant.[12] An alternate way to interpret this passage might be to hear this subdominant harmony as connected to the earlier supertonic harmony (bars 13–16) and the return to the dominant in bar 20 at a more local level. Either way, the fundamental structure remains the same, and it is this structure, not the details of the voice-leading, that links the Sarabande with the previous two movements.

Gigue

While the intervening movements—the Gavotte, Polonaise, Petit Menuet, and Bourrée—may be considered contrasting with occasional references to the earlier movements, the Gigue exhibits clear motivic and structural links to the Prelude and to the opening three movements of the suite. The Gigue also resolves registral completion left open in several of the earlier movements, and in this sense it functions as a true completion as well as a summary of the entire suite.

A striking feature of the Gigue is its opening motive, the triadic arpeggiation, which, in the context of this investigation, might be heard as a reference, indeed an inversion, of the arpeggiation motive of the Prelude, BWV 854/1. Because of the imitative nature of the Gigue, this idea is heard several times. Some of these occurrences are marked in figure 6.8, a voice-leading graph of the movement, by vertical brackets.[13] Another feature of the Gigue that would seem to link it with the Prelude is the harmonic progression of its second part—including the employment of d♮—through bar 38. This progression can be represented as follows:

$$V^{8-}{}_{(\,[^{o}7]\ \mathrm{ii}\,)}{}^{-7}\ I^{\,8-\natural 7}\ IV.$$

This is precisely the progression of the connective phrase in the Prelude leading to the repetition of its first phrase beginning on the subdominant. The difference is that in the Prelude the subdominant is the goal, whereas in the Gigue this progression is embedded within a larger prolongation of the dominant. Finally, it should be noted that the treatment of registers in part two of the Gigue is similar to what we hear in both

Figure 6.8. Gigue

the Prelude and the Allemande. Like the Allemande, the Gigue opens its second part in the upper register (b^2), yet closure, at least initially, is heard most strongly in the lower register (bar 44) with completion confirmed in the upper register in bar 48 (not shown in figure 6.8). Though different, there is a strong parallel here to both the Prelude and the Allemande, both of which close only in the lower register.

Part 1 of the Gigue opens with a closed eight-bar phrase in the tonic prolonging scale degree 8, and in this regard it is similar both to the Allemande and to the Courante, though otherwise different in content. The remainder of the first part is divided into two eight-bar phrases, each ending with a cadence on the dominant. While it might be possible to hear bar 16 as the goal of tonal motion and the following phrase as extension and confirmation of that goal,[14] there are at least two factors that point to bar 24 as the true goal: 1) the less-than-conclusive nature of the harmonized descent in bars 9–16; and 2) the continued sixteenth-note motion at the cadence at bar 16. As shown in figure 6.8, the fundamental line descends from scale degree 8 (bars 1–8) conclusively to scale degree 5 at the cadence in bar 24.

The overall motion of bars 9–16 is a descent of a fifth from f♯^{2} to b^1, internal to which there is a preliminary descent from f♯^{2} to c♯^{2}. The descending fifth prolongs its initiating tone, f♯^{2}. The final phrase of part 1 opens with an ascent from b^1 to e^2, which is introduced as a consonance

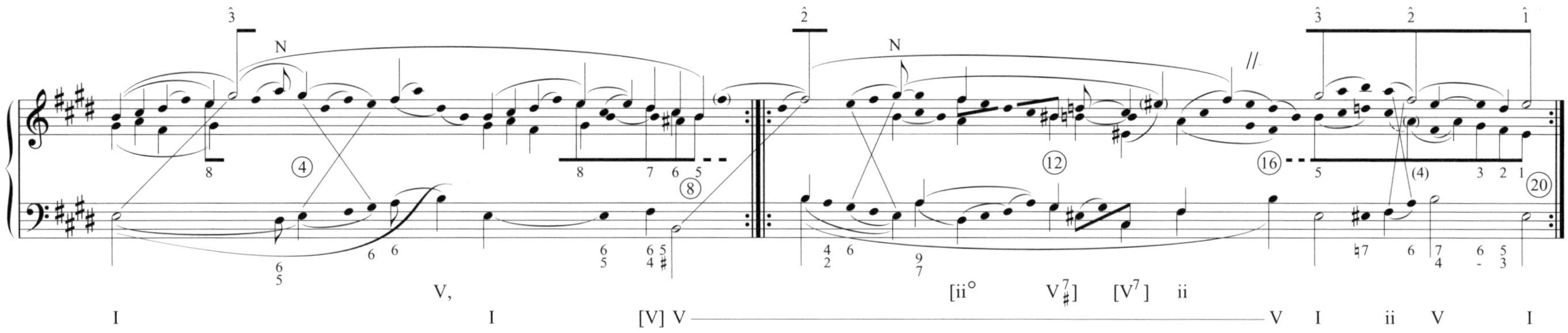

Figure 6.9. Gavotte

before being harmonized as the dissonant seventh of the dominant in the key of the dominant. This e^2 functions as a passing tone connecting the prolonged $f\sharp^2$ of bars 9–16 to scale degree 7 ($d\sharp^2$) of the fundamental line in bar 23.

As noted above, melodic closure—that is, completion of the descent of the octave—occurs in both registers. At bar 44, closure is most clearly heard in the lower register, represented in figure 6.8 by the downward-directed stems and the beam. Closure is clearly implied at this point in the upper register, then confirmed by the following cadence in bar 48. The contents of bars 25–40 are controlled by the dominant harmony supporting the motion 8–7, that is, connecting the b^2 of bar 25 to the a^2 ($\hat{4}$) in bar 40. Internal to this prolonged dominant is the progression described above, which contains its own extended dominant supporting the motion 8–7, in this case in the lower register.

II. The Optional Movements

The four optional movements, like the four standard movements, are structurally related. All have fundamental lines from $\hat{3}$ either continuous or interrupted ($\hat{3}\ \hat{2}//\ \hat{3}\ \hat{2}\hat{1}$). All but the Menuet, which was added later, share one or more characteristics with earlier movements, though these may very well be fortuitous. For the most part, they are different from the standard four, suggesting that they could have been written separately. By contrast, the strong motivic and structural relationships among the standard four and the Prelude suggest they might very well have been conceived as a unit.

Gavotte

A graph of the Gavotte is provided in figure 6.9. Part 1 consists of a modulating period, an antecedent (bars 1–4) answered by a consequent that modulates to the dominant. The first phrase opens with an ascending line leading to scale degree 8 followed immediately by the introduction of the first note of the fundamental line, $g\sharp^2$ ($\hat{3}$). However, in the consequent phrase the ascending motion stops at e^2 and from there descends by step to b^1. The overall motion spanning the two phrases is a descending sixth from $g\sharp^2$ to the inner-voice tone b^1.[15] Only by implication has $\hat{3}$ given way to $\hat{2}$at this point, but the implied $f\sharp^2$ is immediately stated at the outset of part 2 and subsequently prolonged through bar 16 over a dominant harmony. Internal to this passage, d♮, an important element in the previously discussed movements, particularly the

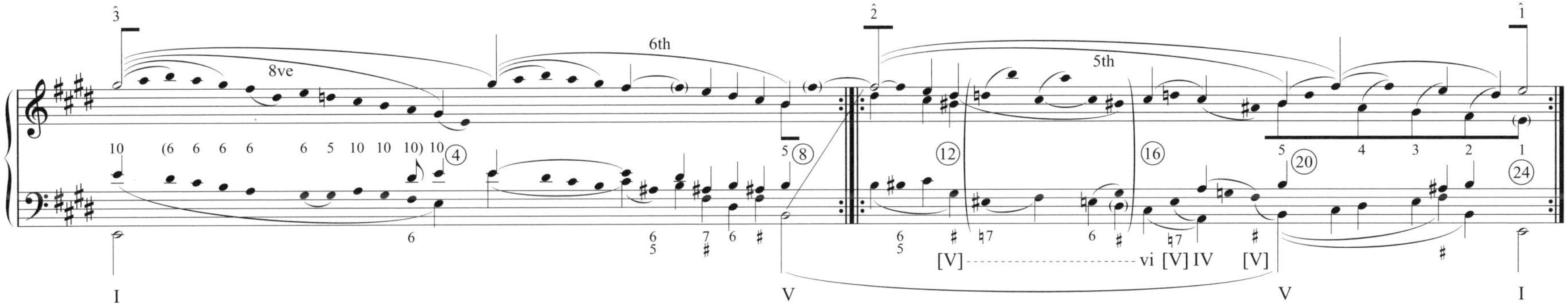

Figure 6.10. Polonaise

Prelude and the Allemande, makes another appearance, here as the dominant of the supertonic harmony. At the modified return to the opening idea, $\hat{3}$ is reinstated and from there the fundamental line descends to closure in the upper register.[16] Meanwhile, in the lower register we hear a clearly articulated descent from b^1 to e^1, completing an octave descent originating in the first part. Once again we have an octave descent encompassing an entire movement (as shown in figure 6.9 by the downward-directed stems and discontinuous beam), reminiscent of what we found in the Prelude.

Polonaise

The Polonaise opens with a closed phrase in the tonic supporting the octave descent $g\sharp^2$–$g\sharp^1$, thereby prolonging the initiating tone ($\hat{3}$) of the fundamental line. As shown in figure 6.10, the consequent phrase descends as far as b^1 at the cadence on the dominant. As in the Gavotte, the fundamental line has descended to $\hat{2}$ only by implication at this point; $f\sharp^2$ is clearly stated, however, at the outset of part 2 and subsequently prolonged until its resolution to closure in the upper register in the final bar of the movement. Part two is divided into two periods, the first leading to a cadence on vi, which is embedded within a longer prolongation of the dominant. The initial phrase of this period leads from the dominant to V of vi, and the second phrase opens with the ubiquitous d♮ as part of a secondary diminished seventh chord leading to an F♯-minor harmony, heard in this context as the subdominant of c♯ minor (vi). This passage is reminiscent of the corresponding passage in the Courante (bars 21–24). The next four bars lead back to the dominant via the subdominant, introduced by its dominant seventh chord (yet another appearance of d♮). The harmonies of bars 9–20 support a stepwise descent from outer voice ($f\sharp^2$) to inner voice (b^1), and, as occurred in the Gavotte, we hear a clearly articulated descent from b^1 to e^1 in an inner voice in these final four bars below resolution of the fundamental line.[17]

Petit Menuet

The Petit Menuet[18] is in rounded binary form, but the return to the opening material in bar 17 does not coincide with a return to tonic harmony, but instead occurs over a prolongation of the dominant. As shown in figure 6.11, scale degree 2 of the fundamental line is prolonged by the octave progression $f\sharp^2$–$f\sharp^1$ leading to closure only in the lower register.[19]

Bourrée

The Bourrée opens with an ascending gesture, an elaborated arpeggiation, leading to $g\sharp^2$ (bar 4), establishing it as the primary tone, and from there the melodic line descends a sixth to b^1 at the cadence on the

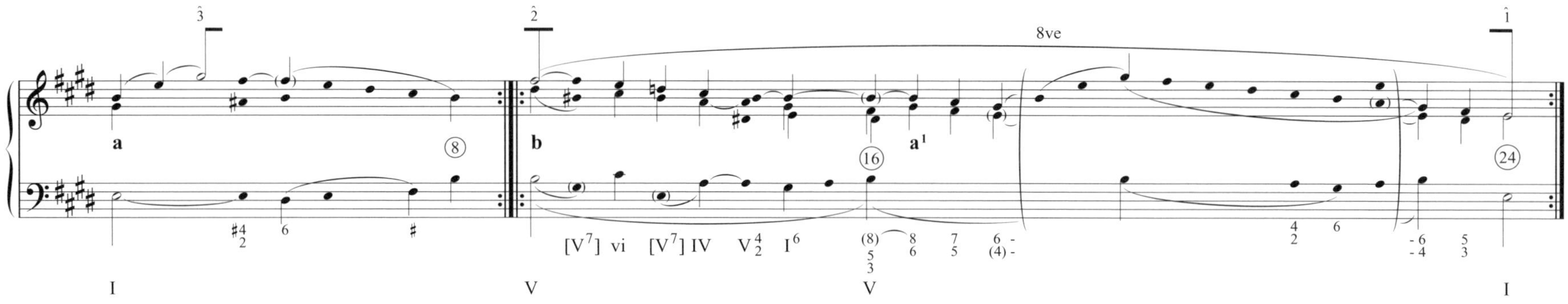

Figure 6.11. Petit Menuet

dominant (bar 12). There are strong parallels here to the other movements in this group. First, in terms of voice-leading, the approach to the primary tone ($\hat{3}$) is analogous to what occurs at the opening of both the Gavotte and the Menuet. Second, the ensuing descending sixth to b^1 parallels what occurs in the opening period of the Gavotte and in the second phrase of the Polonaise. Compare figure 6.12, a graph of the Bourrée, with figures 6.9 (Gavotte, p. 80) and 6.10 (Polonaise, p. 81). As was the case with these other two movements, f♯² ($\hat{2}$) is implied but not stated explicitly at the cadence on the dominant at the end of part 1.

Part 2 presents an interesting analytical question: where to hear the reestablishment of the tonic harmony and g♯² ($\hat{3}$), at bar 29 or at bar 37? I hear the return at bar 29.[20] As shown in figure 6.12, the prolongation of the dominant from the cadence in bar 12 up to this point may be considered, at least in an abstract sense, to support an implied motion (5)–7, internal to which the 5th of the dominant ($\hat{2}$) is displaced by b^2, from which the line descends to f♯² at the cadence on the supertonic (bar 24). It is then from this f♯² that a^2 is introduced by the now familiar arpeggiation figure, first as a consonance, and then, by inference, as the dissonant seventh. Bars 29–37 are interpreted as a prolongation of the tonic harmony and of g♯² by its upper neighbor a^2, a characteristic gesture of the movement at multiple levels. From bar 37 the melodic line descends as if to close in the upper register, but harmonic closure is temporarily avoided, similar to what occurs in bar 29 of the Courante (see figure 6.5, p. 76) and, for that matter, at the end of the Prelude. The primary tone is then reintroduced in the lower register by means of its upper neighbor, from which point closure is finally achieved. As noted above, the task of establishing clear closure in both registers is left to the final movement, the Gigue.

Our investigation of French Suite VI opened with speculation about the possible relationship of the Prelude in E, BWV 854/1, to the Suite, based on its inclusion in Gerber's copy. The compositional links are clear, particularly to the Allemande, Courante and Gigue. From a motivic perspective, the d♮, which plays such an important role in the Prelude, is prominent in the second part of the Allemande, Courante, Sarabande, and Gigue, as well as the Gavotte. And the surface arpeggiation motive appears prominently in the Gigue as well as once at an important structural spot in the Courante. From a structural perspective the encompassing octave descent becomes fundamental to the voice-leading structures of the standard movements.[21] And finally the large-scale arpeggiation e^2–g♯²–b^2 of the Prelude and its harmonization are replicated at more immediate structural levels in the Allemande and Courante, strengthening the links to those two movements. Within the Suite proper, the strongest links are found among the standard four: Allemande, Courante, Sarabande, and Gigue. All these movements are related at the deepest level by sharing the same fundamental structure, and they are also linked motivically. The optional movements also share motivic and structural characteristics, for the most part different from the other four, though one can find a possible link here and there between the two groups. This

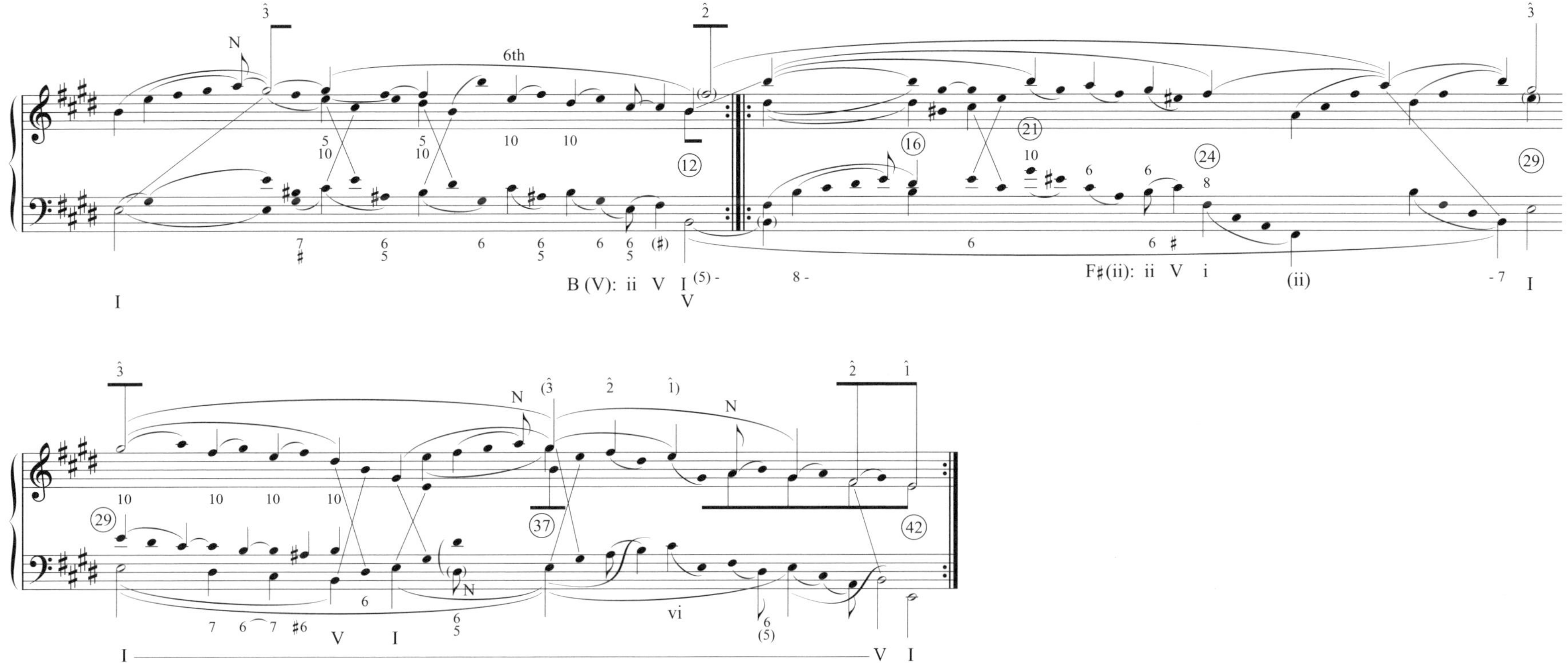

Figure 6.12. Bourrée

raises an interesting possibility, namely that Suite VI, which was assembled separately from the other five in the collection, may have originated from more than one source. No matter what its origins might have been, there can be no doubt that some of its movements are related at multiple levels, suggesting its inclusion, along with others discussed in this study, among those considered as true examples of the variation suite.

Notes

1. The E-major Prelude, along with other preludes later included in *The Well-Tempered Clavier*, originally appeared as a separate movement (item 19) in the *Clavierbüchlein for Wilhelm Friedemann Bach* (1720).

2. Ernst Ludwig Gerber, *Historisch-biographisches Lexicon der Tonkünstler* (Leipzig, 1790–92).

3. Translated in *The New Bach Reader*, ed. Hans T. David and Arthur Mendel, rev. and enlarged Christoph Wolff (W. W. Norton, 1998), 322.

4. My analysis of this work is influenced considerably by ideas conveyed to me years ago by Ernst Oster, with whom I had an opportunity to study this and several other works.

5. This tonal procedure—where the opening motion from the tonic to dominant is answered by a parallel motion progressing from subdominant to a close on the tonic—is rare in baroque music and certainly in Bach's works. It is a procedure found on occasion in classical works and more than occasionally in the works of Franz Schubert.

6. Similar sketches were published in an earlier article, "The Fundamental Line from Scale-Degree 8: Criteria for Evaluation," *Journal of Music Theory* 32, no. 2 (1988): 271–94 (figures 7 and 8). See also Heinrich Schenker, *Free Composition*,

trans. and ed. Ernst Oster (New York: Longman, 1979), figures 76/4, 95/c2, 106/1, 109/d1, and 125/3.

7. Extensions of the cadences at the close of part 1 (bars 8–12) and part 2 (bars 25–28) are not included in figure 6.3 because their contents are not germane to our investigation of inter-movement associations.

8. The primary reason for my differing interpretation of the octave descents in these two movements has to do with the different natures of the seventh degree of the scale. In the Prelude the descent occurs through natural 7 (d♮), whereas in the Allemande it is by means of the diatonic seventh. Furthermore, the arpeggiation to b^2 in the Allemande occurs within a closed phrase in the tonic where the controlling pitch is e^2, whereas this is not the case in the Prelude.

9. cf. Schenker, *Free Composition*, figures 47/3 and 87/1b.

10. Though harmonic closure is not achieved until the very last bar, I have indicated the implied bass on the downbeat of bar 29 to be e and the harmony to be "tonic" in figure 6.5 to show the parallel between the final four bars and the equivalent passage at the end of part 1. There is, of course, an important difference between the two. The last four bars of part 1 extend the local point of arrival, whereas here they are necessary to confirm the delayed point of arrival.

11. Notes and preliminary sketches of this movement by Schenker indicate indecision regarding whether to interpret the fundamental line from the opening g♯^{1} ($\hat{3}$) or the b^1 ($\hat{5}$) in bar 8, though at one point $\hat{3}$is crossed out in favor of ($\hat{5}$). The possibility of an octave line with a suppressed $\hat{8}$, as interpreted here, was not considered. These notes and sketches are contained in The Oster Collection: Papers of Heinrich Schenker, New York Public Library, Music Division, File 69, p. 41 and file 70, pp. 8–11.

12. See Schenker, *Free Composition*, figure 62/9.

13. The arpeggiation motive is represented in figure 6.8 as a chord in order to economize on space.

14. A graph of the Gigue in the hand of Angi Elias (The Oster Collection, file 70, p. 17) indicates a descent of the fundamental line to $\hat{5}$ already in bar 16, though a preliminary graph by Schenker (file 70, p. 25) seems to indicate preference for the more definitive descent in bars 23–24. Though Schenker clearly settles on a reading of the fundamental line from $\hat{8}$, a preliminary sketch (file 70, p. 18) reveals an attempt to read the structure from $\hat{3}$ (g♯^{2}) in bar 8.

15. In a preliminary graph of this movement Schenker indicated a descending fifth progression commencing from the f♯^{2} on the upbeat to bar 4 and the prolongation of the dominant from this dividing cadence, rather than the interpretation given in figure 6.9, which shows this f♯^{2} as part of a descending sixth. (See The Oster Collection, file 70, p. 12.) Schenker is consistent in this regard. See his interpretation of the first part of the Bourrée (file 70, p. 15).

16. The return of the tonic harmony is short-lived. With the addition of d♮ and the simultaneous chromatic change in the bass from e to e♯ the harmony is directed again to the supertonic as preparation for the structural dominant. Though brief, the return to g♯^{2} in conjunction with a return to the opening idea is sufficient, I believe, to warrant this reading of the Gavotte.

17. If closure had occurred only in the lower register, it would be tempting to read the prolongation of $\hat{2}$ by an octave descent f♯^{2} to f♯^{1} leading to e^1, as occurs in part 2 of the Petit Menuet.

18. My placement of the Petit Menuet, which was added at a later date at the end, is based on an assumption that it was most likely intended as a trio to the Polonaise. It is not appropriate as a closing movement.

19. This interpretation differs from the one provided by Schenker in a preliminary sketch (The Oster Collection, file 70, p. 14). Despite the return over a pedal b (six-four chord), Schenker reads an implied tonic harmony in bar 17 (the norm) rather than a continuation of the dominant.

20. Schenker's preliminary graph of this movement (The Oster Collection, file 70, p. 15) clearly indicates the return at bar 37, subsuming the tonic harmony in bar 29 within a larger dominant prolongation (supporting the dissonant seventh) spanning bars 27–36.

21. The prominent role of the octave as a large-scale organizing device in this suite, in the Suite in A minor, BWV 818/818a, and in general in Bach's works points to an interesting question: why do we encounter structural octaves in Bach's music, or for that matter, in late baroque music in general, but not in compositions of the classical period? Perhaps the answer to this question lies in the differing nature of the forms employed. For example, the tonal motion of the typical baroque binary form is continuous, a condition favorable to the large-scale unfolding of octave lines, while classical binary forms (rounded binary and sonata form) involve interruption. For a recent discussion of this and other relevant issues, see David Smyth, "Schenker's Octave Lines Reconsidered," *Journal of Music Theory* 43, no. 1 (1999): 101–33.

Epilogue

It has been my experience over the years that I have been drawn to certain musical works, to listen to them over and over again, and eventually to study them in detail to understand what it is about them that engages me, in essence to understand in concrete terms what my musical intuitions have already grasped. Some of Bach's suites—here I would cite specifically the first two violin partitas; the first, third, and fourth cello suites; and the keyboard partitas—are among this ever-expanding list. What I have found about these and other works to which I have been drawn is that they are particularly rich in harmonic, motivic, and structural associations, and it was curiosity about the extent to which these relationships might be exhibited throughout the forty-four suites that led me to this study. That is, do all the suites exhibit inter-movement connections of the variety I had perceived in, say, the first cello suite and the second violin partita? The answer, of course, is negative. There are some that appear to exhibit no such relationships, some with a variety of discernible connections, and others that exhibit a diverse, and sometimes complex web of inter-movement associations, some easily perceptible but others less obvious except to the trained ear. Personally I am drawn to those in this last group. The more complex the better. But this should not be taken as a value judgment. The baroque suite is a collection of pieces in the same key, and there are many wonderful examples by Bach that are just that. Consider some of the suites I have not discussed, including some of the English and French suites. These too are fantastic works, equally worthy of our attention.

It should not come as a surprise that many of Bach's suites do exhibit inter-movement associations, given the tradition from which he came. He learned his craft in part by studying the music of preceding generations, often copying complete works or making arrangements of them. As noted in chapter one, he made a keyboard arrangement (BWV 965) of the first sonata, actually a partita, from Reincken's *Hortus Musicus* (1687). This is a variation suite, so there can be no doubt that Bach was acquainted with that tradition. Whether or not he was directly acquainted with Niedt's tract on variation technique, in which the author shows how to write an entire suite based on a given figured bass (not unlike basing a succession of movements on a *cantus firmus*, an older tradition) is an open question, though, if he did, he seems not to have adopted this method as a regular means of composing. Rather, the inter-movement connections exhibited in his suites are far more varied and sophisticated than what Niedt proposes, perhaps closer to what we find in the Reincken work.

So what have we discovered in our study of unifying devices in the Bach suites? First, in the harmonic realm, we have found very few examples of movements based on the same figured bass. The only example where this appears to hold throughout is the Allemande–Courante pair from the *Praeludium et Partita del tuono terzo* (BWV 833), and even here one must work a bit to reveal the connections (see figure 1.10, p. 11). Much more common are suites exhibiting the same large-scale harmonic design, though it seems to me that this relationship is greatly strengthened when these common designs are combined with similar mid-level and deep-level voice-leading patterns, as we have observed on several occasions. Having a common fundamental structure is not significant in itself, at least in this context, but takes on greater significance when this occurs in conjunction with other common features, harmonic and/or motivic. However, in this regard, I would suggest that movements from the Keyboard Suite in A Minor (BWV 818a)—the prototypes outlined in figure 5.3 (p. 59)—function almost like *Ur*-motives. In this particular case, the movements are connected at more immediate levels, reinforcing the relationship.

The most fruitful avenue of investigation into inter-movement connections in these works has proven to be the concept of pitch motive defined and developed in chapters three and four. In this regard, it is interesting to note, but not surprising, that the examples of motivic repetition cited from early works, for example from the keyboard suites BWV 820–822, are all very much at the surface of the music, that is, easily recognizable, and though this type of relationship persists to some degree, it would appear that the more complex types of motivic repetitions appear only in the more mature works. We have seen that the single pitch, e.g., the lowered-seventh degree of the scale, can function as a motivic link among movements, either by itself, as in the first keyboard partita (BWV 825), or as part of a larger construct, as in the first English suite (BWV 806) or the fourth cello suite (BWV 1010), and several examples where movements of a suite are related by expanded voice-leading patterns: the flute partita (BWV 1013), the Overture in the French Style (BWV 831), and the first and second violin partitas (BWV 1002 and 1004). In the last two of these works, as in the Keyboard Suite in A Minor (BWV 818a) and in the French Suite in E Major (BWV 817), motivic repetition at various levels is combined with structural similarities at the deepest level of two or more of their movements. The last two works cited are particularly rich in harmonic, motivic, and structural associations at multiple levels, the reason I have singled them out as summary examples.

I would like to close by returning briefly to a question that has been implied at various times in this study, but not yet posed directly: what is a variation suite? Or, more to the point, what are the conditions that must be satisfied to qualify as a variation suite? It seems that the minimal condition is that two or more of its movements must be related throughout. One approach is to limit our view to what contemporary theorists, like Niedt, had to say about musical organization. This view leads inevitably to the conclusion that the only example of a variation suite in Bach's *oeuvre* is the *Praeludium et Partita del tuono terzo,* BWV 833. This is a reasonable conclusion. But I would argue that we should not limit ourselves in this way. The best evidence we have is not writings about music, but the music itself. If we can accept that movements can be related throughout by common harmonic and voice-leading constructs, as I have attempted to demonstrate, and that these relationships are frequently supported by motivic associations, then surely we must include in our list of this genre not only BWV 817 and 818a and the first two violin partitas (BWV 1002 and 1004), but also the fifth English Suite (BWV 810) and perhaps several others whose movements have been shown to be motivically linked.

Appendix
Theoretical Terms and Definitions

Anstieg: A harmonized linear ascent to the primary tone [*Kopfton*], the initial tone of the Fundamental line [*Urlinie*].

Closure: As employed here, this term refers to the completion of harmonic motion to the tonic (harmonic closure) in conjunction with descent of the fundamental line to scale degree one (melodic closure). Closure can occur at different levels, but normally the term, if not specified otherwise (e.g., local closure), refers to completion of the fundamental structure [*Ursatz*].

Fundamental line [*Urlinie*]: In Schenker's theory a stepwise descending line leading from the primary tone [*Kopfton*], always a member of the tonic triad (e.g., scale degree 3, 5, or 8), to closure. The fundamental line is represented in musical graphs or sketches by open (white) notes and by Arabic numerals with carets above.

Graph or Sketch: Representation of an interpretation of musical structure using musical notation, where the note values and other symbols indicate the relative structural significance, not the duration, of events (as opposed to the reduction, where note values do indicate relative duration). There are two types of graphs/sketches employed in this book, one which shows considerable detail and retains bar lines as an aid to readers, and the other which omits details for the sake of representing more clearly structural connections at deeper (more remote) levels. See, for example, figures 6.1 and 6.2, two representations of the structure of the Prelude in E Major (BWV 854/1).

Hypermeter: The regular grouping of bars, normally in multiples of two, where the individuals components, the bars, function at a higher level much the same as beats function within the bar with respect to relative stress. In the suites, hypermeter is most evident in dance movements like the menuet. See, for example, the Menuet from the second French Suite (BWV 813) (figure 1.2), where the prevailing hypermeter is quadruple, corresponding in general to the phrase divisions. Note, however, that the eight-bar phrase beginning in bar 17, which is based on a two-bar sequence, is continuous, not divisible into four plus four. Specific references to hypermetric organization in the suites are listed in the Index.

Primary Tone [*Kopfton*]: The initial tone of the fundamental line.

Reduction: A simplification of the music resulting from elimination of decorative elements. In the reduction, unlike the graph or sketch, note values represent relative duration, not actual duration in the score but duration of control once melodic embellishments and rhythmic displacements are removed. See, for example, the reductions of the opening bars of the Allemanda, Corrente, Sarabande, and Tempo di Borea movements from Violin Partita I (BWV 1002), provided in figure 1.6.

Ursatz: Fundamental structure, consisting of the fundamental line [*Urlinie*] and its harmonic support.

Zug: A linear harmonized progression spanning a specific interval, e.g., a fifth.

Bibliography

Bach, Johann Sebastian. *J. S. Bach's Precepts and Principles for Playing the Thorough-Bass or Accompanying in Four Parts.* [Leipzig, 1738]. Translation with facsimile, introduction, and explanatory notes by Pamela L. Poulin. Oxford: Clarendon Press, 1994.

Beach, David. "The Fundamental Line from Scale-Degree 8: Criteria for Evaluation." *Journal of Music Theory* 32, no. 2 (1988): 271–94.

Beck, Hermann. *The Suite.* Translated by Robert Holben. Cologne: Arno Volk, 1966.

Burkhart, Charles. "Schenker's 'Motivic Parallelisms.'" *Journal of Music Theory* 22, no. 2 (1978): 145–75.

David, Hans T., and Arthur Mendel. *The New Bach Reader.* Revised and expanded by Christoph Wolff. New York: W. W. Norton, 1998.

Fuller, David. "Suite." *The New Grove Dictionary of Music and Musicians,* edited by Stanley Sadie. 2nd edition. 29 vols. New York: Grove, 2001, 24:665–84.

Fuller, David, and Cliff Eisen. "Partita." *The New Grove Dictionary of Music and Musicians,* edited by Stanley Sadie. 2nd edition. 29 vols. New York: Grove, 2001, 19:173–74.

Lester, Joel. *Bach's Works for Solo Violin.* Oxford: Oxford University Press, 1999.

Nelson, Robert U. *The Technique of Variation.* Berkeley and Los Angeles: University of California Press, 1949.

Niedt, Friederich Erhard. *Musikalische Handleitung I: Vom General-Bass* (1700); *II: Handleitung zur Variation* (1706; 2nd expanded edition, ed. J. Mattheson, 1721); *III: Von Contra-Punct, Canon, Motetten, Choral, Recitativ-Stylo, und Cavatten,* ed. J. Mattheson (1717). Translated as *Musical Guide* by Pamela L. Poulin and Irmgard C. Taylor. Oxford: Oxford University Press, 1989.

Rothstein, William. *Phrase Rhythm in Tonal Music.* New York: Schirmer, 1989.

Schachter, Carl. "The Gavotte en Rondeaux from J. S. Bach's Partita in E Major for Unaccompanied Violin." *Israel Studies in Musicology* 4 (1987): 7–26.

Schenker, Heinrich. *Free Composition.* [1935]. Translated and edited by Ernst Oster. New York: Longman, 1979.

———. *The Masterwork in Music.* Edited by William Drabkin, translated by Ian Bent, William Drabkin, Richard Kramer, John Rothgeb, and Hedi Siegel. 3 vols. Cambridge: Cambridge University Press, 1994, 1996 and 1997.

———. Notes and Unpublished Sketches of the French Suite in E Major, BWV 817. The Oster Collection: Papers of Heinrich Schenker, New York Public Library, Music Division, File 69, pp. 37–46, and File 70, pp. 4–25.

Schulenberg, David. "Composition and Improvisation in the School of J. S. Bach." *Bach Perspectives* 1, edited by Russell Stinson (1995): 1–42.

———. "Composition as Variation: Inquiries into the Compositional Procedures of the Bach Circle of Composers." *Current Musicology* 33 (1982): 57–87.

———. *The Keyboard Music of J. S. Bach.* New York: Schirmer, 1992.

Sisman, Elaine. "Variations." *The New Grove Dictionary of Music and Musicians,* edited by Stanley Sadie. 2nd edition. 29 vols. New York: Grove, 2001, 26:284–326.

Smyth, David. "Schenker's Octave Lines Reconsidered." *Journal of Music Theory* 43, no. 1 (1999): 101–33.

Wolff, Christoph. *Bach: Essays on His Life and Music.* Cambridge, MA: Harvard University Press, 1991.

———. *Johann Sebastian Bach: The Learned Musician.* New York: W. W. Norton, 2000.

Wolff, Christoph, Walter Emery, Ulrich Leisinger, Stephen Roe, and Peter Wollny. "Johann Sebastian Bach." *The New Grove Dictionary of Music and Musicians,* edited by Stanley Sadie. 2nd edition. 29 vols. New York: Grove, 2001, 2:309–82.

Index

Altnickol, Johann Christoph, 71

Bach, Carl Philipp Emanuel, 9, 12n11
Bach, Johann Nicolaus, 8–9
Bach, Johann Sebastian:
  BWV 766–768, *Partite diverse*, xiiin1, 8
  BWV 806, English Suite I, 8, 12n3, 28–29, 34, 38n6, 86
  BWV 807, English Suite II, 8, 12n3
  BWV 808, English Suite III, 8, 12n3
  BWV 810, English Suite V, 22–24, 52n1, 86
  BWV 811, English Suite VI, 6–7, 8, 12n3, 25n7
  BWV 812, French Suite I, 57
  BWV 813, French Suite II, 4–5, 27
  BWV 816, French Suite V, 4, 25n7
  BWV 817, French Suite VI, xii, 4, 52, 69n5, 71–84, 86
  BWV 818/818a, Keyboard Suite in A Minor, xii, 5–6, 8, 12n3, 29, 52, 57–69, 77, 84n21, 85, 86
  BWV 820, Overture in F Major, 30, 31, 38n7, 85
  BWV 821, Keyboard Suite in B-flat, 30, 85
  BWV 822, Keyboard Suite in G Minor, 30–31, 32, 38n8, 85
  BWV 825, Partita I, 15–17, 18, 19, 20, 25n3, 28, 34, 38n5, 86
  BWV 826, Partita II, 12n1, 15, 16, 17, 24n1, 25n7, 29–30
  BWV 827, Partita III, 12n1, 27–28, 38n4
  BWV 828, Partita IV, 32, 34, 35
  BWV 829, Partita V, 3, 17, 19, 20, 21, 25n4, 38n12
  BWV 830, Partita VI, 3–4, 12n1, 25n7, 27
  BWV 831, Overture in the French Style, 40–43, 86
  BWV 833, *Prelude et Partita del tuono terzo*, xii, 10–11, 12n3, 15, 27–28, 85, 86
  BWV 854/1, Prelude in E Major, *Well-Tempered Clavier* I, 71–74, 75, 76, 77, 78, 79, 80, 81, 82, 83n1
  BWV 940, Little Prelude in D Minor, 69n2
  BWV 942, Little Prelude in A Minor, 69n2
  BWV 965, Keyboard Arrangement of Sonata I from Reincken's *Hortus musicus*, 9–10, 85
  BWV 996, Lute Suite II, 27
  BWV 997, Lute Suite III, 8, 12n3
  BWV 1002, Violin Partita I, 6–8, 12n3, 43–46, 86
  BWV 1004, Violin Partita II, 12n3, 46–51, 52, 53n10, 86
  BWV 1007, Cello Suite I, 31–32, 33, 38n9
  BWV 1009, Cello Suite III, 19, 21–22, 25n5, 25n6
  BWV 1010, Cello Suite IV, 34–36, 38n10, 38n11, 86
  BWV 1013, Flute Partita, 4, 39–40, 52n2, 52n3, 52n4, 52n5
  BWV 1066, Orchestral Suite I, 4, 25n7, 30, 31, 35, 37
  BWV 1067, Orchestral Suite II, 12n3, 12n6
  Clavierbüchlein für Anna Magdalena Bach, 71
  Clavier-Büchlein für Wilhelm Friedemann Bach, 83n1
  Gründlicher Unterricht des General-Basses, 9
  Well-Tempered Clavier I, 71, 74, 83n1
Beck, Hermann, xiiin2
Beethoven, Ludwig, Fifth Symphony, 27
Böhm, Georg, xii
Burkhart, Charles, 38n1, 38n3
Buxtehude, Dietrich, *Auf meinen lieben Gott* (BUXWV 179), 8, 12n8

David, Hans T., 12n11, 83n3
Derr, Ellwood, xiiin3
double, 5–8, 12n3, 12n6, 12n7, 38n6
Drabkin, William, 25n6, 69n2

Elias, Angi, 84n14

Forkel, Johann Nikolaus, 12n11
form: of Praeambulum, Partita V, 3; of Toccata, Partita VI, 3–4; of Menuet, French Suite II, 4–5, 6: rounded binary, 4, 52n4
Froberger, Johann Jacob, xii
Fuller, David, xiiin2, 38n9

Gerber, Ernst Ludwig, *Historisch-biographisches Lexicon der Tonkünstler*, 71, 83n2
Gerber, Heinrich Nicolaus, 57, 71, 82

Handel, George Frideric, xii, 12n7
hypermeter: Flute Partita (BWV 1013), 40 (Figure 4.2), 52n3; Keyboard Suite in A Minor (BWV 818), Sarabande simple, 65 (Figure 5.10); Keyboard Suite in A Minor (BWV 818a), Sarabande, 64 (Figure 5.9); Keyboard Suite in G Minor (BWV 822), Overture, 32 (Figure 3.9), 38n8; Violin Partita II (BWV 1004), Sarabande, 53n10. *See also* metric reinterpretation; parenthetical digression; phrase expansion

Kirnberger, Johann Philipp, 9, 13n11
Kuhnau, Johann, xii

Laufer, Edward, 53n8
Lester, Joel, 53n7, 53n9

Mendel, Arthur, 83n3
metric reinterpretation: French Suite VI (BWV 817), Courante, 76 (Figure 6.5), 77. *See also* hypermeter
motive: definition of different types, 27, 39; form-defining role of, 3–5; motivic parallels, 27–37 *passim*

Niedt, Friederich Erhard, *Musicalische Handleitung II: Handleitung zur Variation*, 8–9, 12n9, 13n13, 85, 86

octave progressions: Cello Suite IV (BWV 1010), 34, 35, 36 (Figure 3.14); French Suite VI (BWV 817), 74–80 (Figures 6.3–6.8), 84n21; Keyboard Suite in A Minor (BWV 818/818a), 59–69 (Figures 5.3–5.8; 5.10–5.14); Orchestral Suite I (BWV 1066), 35, 37 (Figure 3.16); Partita V (BWV 829), 19, 20 (Figure 2.8), 21 (Figure 2.9), 38n12; Prelude in E Major (BWV 854/1), 73 (Figure 6.2)
Oster, Ernst, 83n4, 84n6
Oster Collection (New York Public Library), 84n11, 84n14, 84n15, 84n19, 84n20

parenthetical digression: Cello Suite III (BWV 1009), Gigue, 21, 22 (Figure 2.11); Keyboard Suite in A Minor (BWV 818a), Prelude, 59, 60 (Figure 5.4); Partita II (BWV 826), Allemande and Courante, 15, 17 (Figure 2.2); Partita V (BWV 829), Sarabande, 25n4. *See also* hypermeter; phrase expansion
phrase expansion: Flute Partita (BWV 1013), Bourrée, 40 (Figure 4.2); Partita V (BWV 829), Sarabande, 25n4. *See also* parenthetical digression
Poulin, Pamela, 12n9, 13n13

Reincken, Johann Adam, xii; *Hortus musicus*, Sonata I, 9–10, 85
repetition, role of, 3–8 *passim*
Rothstein, William, 52n3

Schenker, Heinrich, 22, 27, 35, 38n1, 38n3, 39, 53n6, 84n11, 84n14, 84n15, 84n19, 84n20; *Free Composition*, 69n2, 84n6, 84n9, 84n12; *The Masterwork in Composition*, 25n6, 69n2; Schenkerian graphs, xii, xiiin6
Schubert, Franz, 83n5
Schulenberg, David, xi, xiiin2, xiiin4, xiiin5, 9, 10, 11, 12n10, 13n14, 13n15, 38n7, 57, 69n1
seventh degree of the scale lowered (flat 7); Cello Suite IV (BWV 1010), 34–36, 38n11; English Suite I (BWV 806), 28–29; Partita I (BWV 825), 15–17, 28, 34, 38n6; Partita V (BWV 829), 19, 20 (Figure 2.8), 21 (Figure 2.9)
Siegel, Heidi, 25n6, 69n2
Sisman, Elaine, 10, 13n14
Smyth, David, 84n21
Stinson, Russell, xiiin2, 12n10
style, consistency of, xi

Taylor, Imgard C., 12n9

unity, xi–xii, 3, 8, 85–86

variation suite, xii, 8–11, 83, 85, 86
variation technique, role of, 3–8 *passim*

Wolff, Christoph, xi, xiiin4, 12n11, 83n3

Aspects of Unity in J. S. Bach's Partitas and Suites

David W. Beach

Musicians—listeners, performers, and scholars alike—have often felt a profound connectedness between various movements in multimovement works by the great composers. But sensing musical unity is one thing; showing it is another.

In *Aspects of Unity in J. S. Bach's Partitas and Suites,* David Beach examines many of the forty-four works by Bach in this genre for keyboard, orchestra, and solo instruments, including the beloved solo works for violin and for cello from this perspective.

Through careful attention to motivic and harmonic repetitions at various structural levels, made plain to the eye in numerous annotated musical examples and diagrams, Beach establishes that Bach often did link several movements of a suite in various ways, sometimes by overt but often by more subtle means. *Aspects of Unity in J. S. Bach's Partitas and Suites* thus provides new insight into the inner workings of these great pieces.

David W. Beach is a renowned music analyst and historian of music theory who recently retired as Dean of the Faculty of Music, University of Toronto. He co-translated Kirnberger's *The Art of Musical Strict Composition* and edited *Aspects of Schenkerian Theory* (both for Yale University Press) and is co-editor of *Music Theory in Concept and Practice* (Eastman Studies in Music, University of Rochester Press).

"This intense investigation of suites by J. S. Bach reveals his profound and prolific invention, of a kind that has fascinated composers, performers, and theorists for nearly three centuries. Beach is the ideal connoisseur to lead us through this creative maze, with his intimate knowledge of the music, his sensitive musical perception, and a rare gift for truly lucid analytical explanation."

—Jonathan Dunsby, founding editor of *Music Analysis* and Professor of Music, University of Reading

"This book, with its meticulous analytical graphs and learned interpretations based upon many years of study, is certain to be of great interest to Bach scholars and to students of music in general."

—Allen Forte, Battell Professor of Music Theory, Yale University

"An insightful study of inter-movement connections in the Bach Suites—some of the greatest multi-movement works ever composed. An important contribution to the scholarly literature."

—Carl Schachter, Distinguished Professor Emeritus of Music, CUNY, and author of *Unfoldings: Essays in Schenkerian Theory and Analysis*